HANCOCK SHAKER VILLAGE

A Guidebook and History

by John Harlow Ott

Fourth Edition

Library of Congress Catalog Card Number 76-19117
ISBN 0-917322-00-2

Printed in the United States of America

Book design by Philip Lief

This book is respectfully dedicated to the men and women who comprised the Hancock Shaker Community during its one hundred and seventy years of spiritual and temporal life.

Table of Contents

Guide

Introduction

No publication can be of more importance to visitors to Hancock Shaker Village than this history and guide by John H. Ott. The trustees of Shaker Community, Inc., have long felt the need for such a publication in order to give visitors the origins of the Shaker movement and some sense of American society into which the Shaker order was planted, prospered and later lost its sustaining force. Life here at "the City of Peace," as Hancock was called, will be better understood and appreciated as a result of reading this useful and comprehensive guide.

Research for this book began soon after Mr. Ott joined the Village staff, first as its curator in 1970 and then, as director in 1972. Data uncovered became the material for the thesis of his Master of Arts Degree in American History Museum Training awarded by the State University of New York at Oneonta and the New York State Historical Association at Cooperstown. While writing the guide was stimulated by a professional motivation, none who witnessed his enthusiasm and persistence could doubt that it was truly a labor of love. It also has the discipline of a work which had to meet the test of accuracy and original research.

Many records, maps, deeds, prints, and photographs are pictured here for the first time. Added to these are personal recollections of friends and neighbors of the Shakers and some who lived with them, which gives the Hancock story life and vitality. Discovered too late for inclusion in Mr. Ott's manuscript is a bit of Hancock Shakerana dating from 1835. It was the occasion of General Lafayette's triumphant tour of America. On his route from Albany to Boston, the general stopped briefly in Pittsfield and was accorded a reception by the town's notables. *The Pittsfield Sun* of June 23, 1835, noted that "in the crowd were some of the leaders of our celebrated (Hancock) Shakers, who, contrary to their custom, approached the august personage with *their hats in hand*".

At the time of writing the history of Hancock, Mr. Ott was involved in directing the work of restoring important buildings, reclaiming many acres of pasture and woodland, and re-establishing and stocking the working farm. This required meticulous research into the past and uncovered priceless data. In this way, Mr. Ott was able to ascertain the various uses and functions of most of the buildings and rooms within them.

In this 200th anniversary year of the founding of Hancock Shaker Village, it is appropriate to have an updated edition of this guidebook and history, marking also thirty years of restoration, renewal and progress of our beloved village. It has proved to be useful to visitors numbering in the hundreds of thousands since opening day July 3, 1961.

Now it is time to strengthen our commitments which were stated quite simply by our Trustees in 1960; "The acquisitions of these buildings with some 1,000 acres of land represents the first successful attempt to save for the future a complete Shaker settlement open to the general public with a unique program of conserving the land, buildings, artifacts and values of an unusually significant way of life and work."

"Through seminars, lectures, exhibitions, tours, publications and other means the community will encourage and provide facilities for a broad program in the humanities, envisaged as a center for study and scholarly research in American communal history cooperating with schools, colleges, libraries, museums and historical societies."

Two hundred years of Shaker life in this lovely village has left us a fascinating legacy. With this history and guide we expect our visitors to become ever more familiar with the Believers' customs and order, their discipline, the vitality of their thought, their pursuit of perfection and their consecration to God. In learning more comes the realization that many facets of their life are relevant and useful today. Their style was strong and simple, an example of Christianity unencumbered by pretense. A favorite little song of Fanny Estabrook, the last Eldress at Hancock, expresses what she felt about the Shakers and their duty:

Our tools are kind and gentle words,
Our shop is in the heart,
And here we manufacture peace,
That we may such impart.

Amy Bess Miller
Hancock Shaker Village
March 28, 1990

Wood engraving from Barber's Historical Collections of Every Town in Massachusetts, 1839

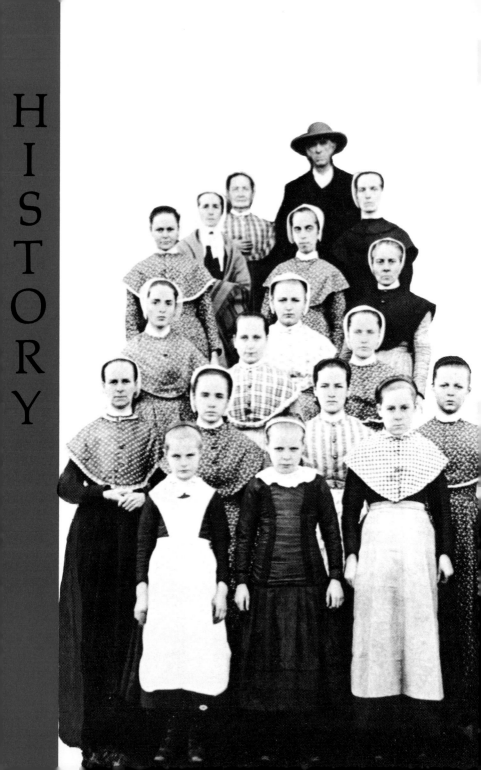

I

Founding of the Shaker Movement

In Manchester, England, in 1747, a small group of Quakers led by James and Jane Wardley formed a separate religious society based upon the Quaker beliefs of meekness, simplicity, and pacifism, and adopted the seizures, trances, and dancing practiced by the Camisards or French Prophets. They evolved their own patterns of worship, which led to their being derisively called Shaking Quakers and later Shakers. Their testimony was close to that of the early Christian church which, through visions and revelations, "testified that Christ the anointed Savior was at hand and the Church was rising in full glory and would increase till every living promise was fulfilled."

Ann Lee, the 23 year old daughter of a poor blacksmith, came under the influence of this new society. "Ann readily embraced their testimony, and united herself to the society in the month of September, 1758 . . . She was baptized into the same spirit, and by degrees, attained to the full knowledge and experience in spiritual things which they had found," Under parental pressure she had earlier married Abraham Standley, a blacksmith like her father. Four children were born to this marriage, but each had died in infancy which she had interpreted as a sign of God's displeasure. Ann prayed and wrestled with her soul looking for a clear revelation of what all this meant. Finally, God spoke to her and two primary tenets were revealed. The first was the duality of the godhead; God was both father and mother to mankind; a god with two natures, masculine and feminine, with each function distinct in itself, yet one in being. The second was the revelation that the purity and righteousness of man were lost through Adam and Eve in their original sin, namely the practice and self-indulgent use of sexual relations, not the union as a natural act for the propagation of man, but rather as an act of self-gratification. Thus Ann Lee saw God's will pure and undefiled, free from original sin. Members of the society soon realized that Ann was no ordinary convert; her revelations and her very countenance betokened the presence of the Christ spirit. Following her release from prison on a spurious charge of blasphemy in 1770, the members could no longer deny her new state and that she was God's messenger — the holy anointed called to lead them. From this time "Mother Ann", as she was now called, by common acclaim became the leader of the society.

Through these new revelations and her teachings, the established Church of England saw a threat in her unchecked activities. Moreover, their meetings,

Members of the Church Family [c. 1890-1891]

"Shakers near Lebanon state of N York, their mode of worship. Drawn from Life." By Anthony Imbert circa. 1830.

held in the homes of members, had become noisy because the vigorous, unconventional singing and dancing peculiar to this sect were disturbing to the peace. Persecutions began and continued until Mother Ann was again jailed as were others of the group. During this imprisonment, God revealed his plan for her to take her group of believers to America where in time their beliefs would flourish.

On May 9, 1774, Ann Lee with her husband, brother, and six other followers set sail from Liverpool and after a difficult and hazardous voyage landed in New York on August 6th. The group was separated for about a year as each of the members earned a living and preparations were made to move to the newly acquired land at Niskayuna in the woods near Albany, New York. By the middle of 1776 the group was together again and living in a few hastily constructed log cabins at the new community and preparing for the spread of the Gospel. The spread of the Gospel, however, was not to take place for a few years; so the small band cleared land, planted and harvested crops, and improved their structures in preparation for the anticipated influx of new Believers.

At the end of 1779, a religious revival began in New Lebanon, New York, among the New Light Baptists which soon spread throughout the countryside. It was believed that the Millenium was at hand. As the waiting period became more drawn out, religious enthusiasm ebbed; disillusion and despondency set in, and the stage was set for Mother Ann's gospel to fill the void. She and other Shakers believed that the Millenium had already arrived, and as the New Lebanon group learned of the Shaker settlement in the wilderness, they flocked to hear the teachings of Mother Ann and her followers.

News of the sect penetrated the sparsely settled countryside by word of mouth, and by June, 1780, the small community was inundated with great numbers of people who came to listen and ask questions. Many of the inquirers were converted. Confession of sin, vows of celibacy, and obedience to the Society accompanied the conversion process.

Mother Ann was encouraged by the steadily increasing conversions, and in 1781, she and a few followers set out on a missionary journey which lasted until August 1783, preaching the Gospel in the towns and villages of Connecticut and Massachusetts.

During this journey they suffered severe persecutions everywhere, but converts were steadily attracted. Some disaffected Baptists even traveled from Maine and New Hampshire to Harvard, Massachusetts, to witness this new phenomenon and later to embrace the

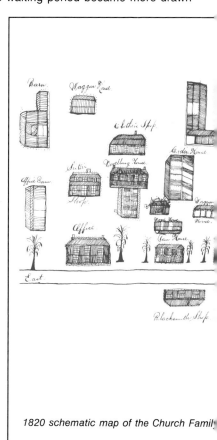

1820 schematic map of the Church Family

Gospel. After two years of preaching and converting, Mother Ann and the elders arrived at the home of Samuel Fitch in Richmond, Massachusetts, where Believers from Pittsfield, Hancock, and Richmond had gathered for their first meeting. On August 3rd, a later meeting was held at the home of Daniel Goodrich Sr. in Hancock (whose house was on the present site of the Village Trustees' House). During the service a mob, having heard that Mother Ann was in the area, was led to the Goodrich farm by Valentine Rathbun Sr., a Baptist minister and influential man in local and state politics. A few years before he had enthusiastically accepted the call of the Shakers and joined, bringing along many members of his congregation and relatives. When his leadership in the sect failed to be recognized, Rathbun left the Society and became one of the earliest and most articulate critics and a bitter antagonist of the Shakers. Supposedly outraged by the Shaker mode of worship, the mob beat and harassed Mother Ann and her followers, forcing them to flee back to Samuel Fitch's house in Richmond. Served with a warrant for disturbing the peace and ordered to leave the area, Ann refused compliance, and her local hosts were jailed. On August 23rd, Mother Ann and her group left for New Lebanon, ending her month long visit in the Hancock area. The future establishment of the Hancock community had begun.

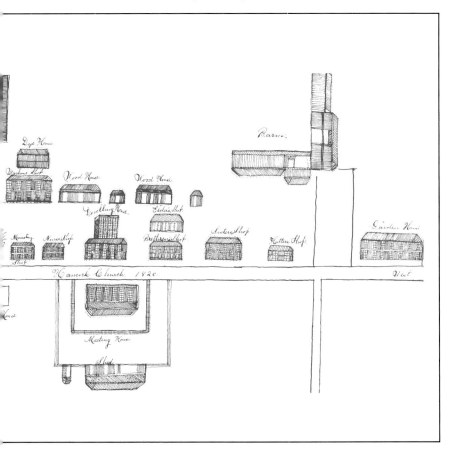

II

Early Growth and Organization

A fter Mother Ann's visit, the small band at Hancock continued to grow. Meeting in the homes of its various members, the group's devotion was typified by the testimony of Amos Rathbun. "I took father, mother, wife, and children, house and land, and all that was dear to me in this world, and put them in one scale, and my soul into the other, and I quick found out which balanced; my soul was my all, and obedience to Mother was my salvation and promise of eternal life."

The nucleus of the Hancock community, the Goodrichs, Demings, Tallcotts, and a few others, had by 1783 consecrated their possessions and lands to the Shaker cause. By August 1784, the young Believers at Hancock and West Pittsfield had begun to lay the foundation for the first meeting house, only a short distance from the home of Daniel Goodrich.

After the death of Mother Ann on September 8, 1784, the seat of spiritual authority of the Shaker Society was moved from Watervliet (Niskayuna) to New Lebanon. Mother Ann's choice as her successor was Father James Whittaker, an English disciple, who continued her missionary work which resulted in great numbers of new converts and the consolidation of scattered Believers into future communities. Elder Joseph Meacham succeeded as the first American born leader in 1787. Father James' "instructions to Elder Joseph Meacham and those with him, relative to gathering, building and establishing the church in Gospel order, might, with great propriety, be likened to the instructions of David to Solomon, concerning the building of the temple, which was an eminent type of this very work." By September 1787, Elder Joseph had completed the first gathering of the Society at New Lebanon and before his death had formalized Shaker doctrine and organization. Although community of goods had been practiced and records kept of the possessions and lands that members contributed to the sect, only verbal covenants existed. Under Meacham the first written covenant was executed in 1795; it specified that "joint interest" or the holding of goods in common was a prerequisite of membership.

In 1790, Father Joseph dispatched Henry Clough and two assistants to bring the Believers at Hancock into the Gospel order since he saw that they were fully committed to God's work. Elder Henry was unsure about assuming the leadership of the new community, and dicussed his doubts with Father Joseph who advised him to speak with several of the other brethren to see if one of them would, in Elder Henry's mind, be a better choice as leader. When he spoke with Calvin

875 view of the Church Family looking east

Harlow, he felt a sense of relief which he interpreted as a sign that Calvin should be appointed. On December 17, 1790, with Father Joseph's approval, Calvin Harlow became Hancock's first bishop, in charge of the Believers in Enfield, Connecticut, as well.

His leadership fulfilled the prophecy of Mother Ann, spoken to Father James Whittaker at Watervliet after her return in 1783. "Calvin is an Elder. O, the bright glories I see for Calvin! I see him stand with the people, like a bishop, ministering the gifts of God." Shortly afterwards on January 1, 1791, Sarah Harrison was appointed as Eldress over the order of sisters to stand with Calvin Harlow. Believers had been gathered into the order of the Church and called the "Church of Hancock" by the beginning of 1791. The term Church was defined as "being a collective body of Christians separated from the world and enjoying, in their united capacity, one common interest."

There were members who, while anxious to follow in the ways of God's work, were hindered in doing so by various financial or personal problems. As a result, other orders or families had to be established. The families were generally located adjacent to the Church Family and named North, East, South, West, depending on their geographic location relative to the Church. Those families located between were called Second or Middle. Each family was a self-contained unit, financially independent, with a subordinate religious role to the Church Family. The lowest order of Shaker was the Novitiate order which at Hancock was housed at the East Family with overflow members at the South Family. Here new members resided either during a trial period or until they had freed themselves from entanglements with worldly problems.

The next level, the Junior order, generally served single members, who had never been married, and those who still wanted some control over their financial or business concerns. Both the Novitiate order and the Junior order could share in the benefits of a united inheritance but retain the rights of family and property before each member decided whether to join the Shaker Society or depart.

The Senior order, or Church Family, constituted the highest level of Shakerism. The individuals in this order had made a total commitment to the Shaker Society and had relinquished all possessions, land, money, and all personal family ties for the benefit of the Society as a whole.

By October 2, 1793, the gathering of families at Hancock was noted in a journal which began: "this is a record of the time of the gathering of the family at the East House together with what they brought with them individually." The East Family was to become the Novitiate order, and the gathering of this family had already been preceded by that of the Second Family in 1792, and that of the West Family in the same year. These gatherings were in the form of verbal agreements.

Several of the major principles of Shakerism were formulated during this time which expanded the tenets of Mother Ann and laid the foundations for the entire body of Shaker belief and practices still followed today.

Highway map and view of Hancock East Family in the 1890's

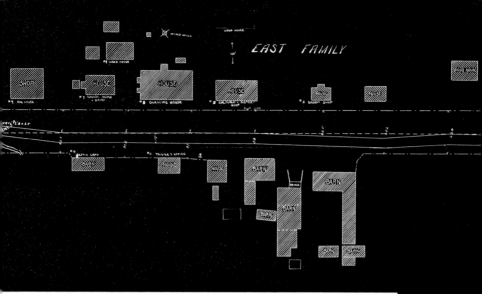

EAST FAMILY

GOVERNMENT AND ORGANIZATION
OF THE HANCOCK COMMUNITY AND CHURCH FAMILY

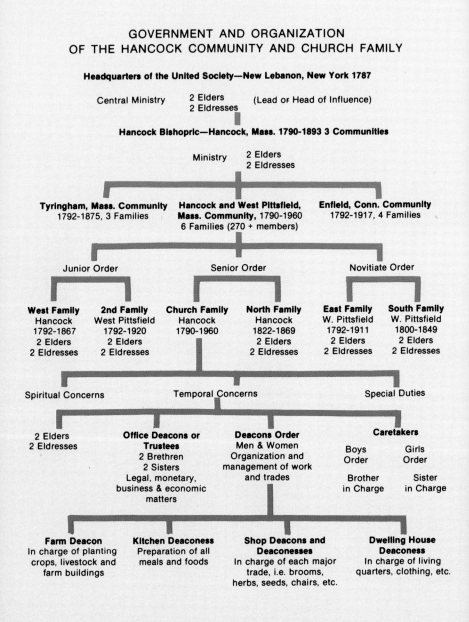

Headquarters of the United Society—New Lebanon, New York 1787

Central Ministry — 2 Elders / 2 Eldresses — (Lead or Head of Influence)

Hancock Bishopric—Hancock, Mass. 1790-1893 3 Communities

Ministry — 2 Elders / 2 Eldresses

Tyringham, Mass. Community
1792-1875, 3 Families

Hancock and West Pittsfield, Mass. Community, 1790-1960
6 Families (270 + members)

Enfield, Conn. Community
1792-1917, 4 Families

Junior Order — Senior Order — Novitiate Order

West Family
Hancock
1792-1867
2 Elders
2 Eldresses

2nd Family
West Pittsfield
1792-1920
2 Elders
2 Eldresses

Church Family
Hancock
1790-1960

North Family
Hancock
1822-1869
2 Elders
2 Eldresses

East Family
W. Pittsfield
1792-1911
2 Elders
2 Eldresses

South Family
W. Pittsfield
1800-1849
2 Elders
2 Eldresses

Spiritual Concerns — Temporal Concerns — Special Duties

2 Elders
2 Eldresses

Office Deacons or Trustees
2 Brethren
2 Sisters
Legal, monetary,
business & economic
matters

Deacons Order
Men & Women
Organization and
management of work
and trades

Caretakers

Boys
Order

Girls
Order

Brother
in Charge

Sister
in Charge

Farm Deacon
In charge of planting
crops, livestock and
farm buildings

Kitchen Deaconess
Preparation of all
meals and foods

**Shop Deacons and
Deaconesses**
In charge of each major
trade, i.e. brooms,
herbs, seeds, chairs, etc.

**Dwelling House
Deaconess**
In charge of living
quarters, clothing, etc.

First was the principle of equality of the sexes in work responsibilities, governing of the families, and in holding positions of trust, such as the duties of office deacon/deaconess in supervising the handling of money and trade. The various levels of responsibility were to be shared by two men and two women. Second, complete separation from the "world" must be practiced. The term "world" represents all people who were not Shakers and all lands and belongings not owned by the Shakers. Third, following Mother Ann's rule of celibacy, a steadfast position separating the sexes in all aspects of communal life and work was rigidly enforced. Finally, the various offices or hierarchy of authority were set forth, whereby the positions of ministers, elders, and deacons were firmly established. Ministers were appointed to oversee both spiritual and temporal needs of the communities under their care. Elders did the same within the confines of the particular families under their charge, and the deacons oversaw temporal affairs such as a particular trade, department, or operation necessary to the well-being of a family.

Growth at Hancock continued slowly but steadily during the Harlow-Harrison years, but Elder Calvin's death on December 20, 1795, followed by that of Eldress Sarah in September 1796, saw the emergence of two new leaders. Elder Nathaniel Deming, who had been Elder Calvin's associate since November 1793, became first in the Hancock ministry with Eldress Casandana Goodrich standing opposite in the sisters' order. From this point on, the expansion of the Church and adjacent families would continue unfailingly.

The membership of the Hancock community seemed to level off after 1783, but many new names were recorded in a journal of the Church Family from 1789 to 1801. During April 1789 alone, five substantial additions to the Society are recorded: Stephen Slosson, a joiner; Josiah Tallcott with numerous tools, who was probably a joiner or cabinetmaker; Hezekiah Osborn, the tax collector for the Town of Hancock and a stone mason; Reuben Rathbun, who later became an elder and was influential in the community before his apostasy; and Jonathan Southwick, a farmer with considerable livestock. It should be noted that during May of the previous year Daniel Goodrich, on behalf of himself and others in the sect, submitted the first of numerous petitions to various state legislatures asking exemption from military service on the ground that their pacifistic religious beliefs forbade military service.

During these early years of growth, living conditions were far from those that marked Hancock's later years. One sister, Rebecca Clark, at the age of eighty-five, recalled her early days at Hancock.

In the year 1791, at the age of 21 I was gathered into the Church at Hancock, Mass....There were nearly a hundred in the family where I lived. When the shell was sounded (a token to rise in the morning) we all quickly rose; and we had but fifteen minutes to dress and get ready for meeting. Fourteen of us slept in one room. When we arose, some packed the beds on one another; some swept the room; others got water to wash in. After our morning meeting, we went to our several employments. Some to getting breakfast for the brethren, as they ate first. Our buildings were small and we had to eat and live accordingly. We worked diligently, early and late, and lived sparingly. Our beds, bedding, and clothing that we brought with us, we all divided among the members of the family, as equally as could

*Door latch system from the
1830 Church Family Dwelling House*

One of the many confections offered for sale by the Shaker Store.

be. We had but few feather beds, our beds were mostly straw; and we made them on the floor. Many of us slept three on one bed; and when we washed our bedding, we had to dry it the same day, and put it on at night. We were all much engaged to build buildings, and to raise provisions, and gather a substance to live on. While the brethren were building, the sisters worked much out of doors to help the brethren. The remainder of the time we were diligent in spinning, weaving, etc., etc. We manufactured all our own clothing for many years; even our caps and handkerchiefs we spun and wove for a number of years.

THE COVENANT

OF THE

Church at Hancock,

To which is prefixed,

A concise Statement of the Faith and principles upon which the joint Union and covenant Relation of Believers are formed; the Nature
of that Relation, and the Order and Manner of attaining and entering into it.

By Order of the Church.

1814.

Our food was very scanty, but what we had we ate with thankful hearts: For breakfast and supper, we lived mostly upon bean porridge and water porridge. Monday morning we had a little weak tea, and once a week a small piece of cheese. Wheat bread was very scarce; and when we had butter it was spread on our bread before we came to the table. Our bread was made chiefly of rye and Indian meal mixed together. Our dinners were generally boiled. Once in a while we had a little milk, but this was a great rarity. When I look back to those days, and then to the fullness with which we are blessed, it fills me with thankfulness.

Solidification of the community was finally completed when the members of the Church entered into their first written covenant in 1796, copied after the New Lebanon covenant of 1795. Covenant members "agree to devote themselves and services, with all that they possess, to the Service of God and the support of the Gospel forever, solemnly promising never to bring debt nor damage, claim nor demand, against the Society, nor against any member thereof, for any property or service which they have devoted to the uses and purposes of the institution." This provision of the covenant is given in its final form and represents the original agreement of 1796, revised in 1801, 1814, and 1830.

(left) Title page of 1814 Church Family Covenant
Original Hancock Meeting House (built by Moses Johnson in 1786) after 1873 alteration

Hancock's situation shortly after the turn of the century looked very promising. Daniel Goodrich notes, in his book of records, that by 1803, there were five families fully established, totaling 142 persons, of whom 76 were in the Church Family. Elder Nathaniel Deming and Eldress Casandana Goodrich must have been pleased with the rapid growth and apparent means of the Society. When the brethren from Hancock and New Lebanon left on their first mission to the West (Ohio and Kentucky) on January 1, 1805, one hundred dollars was contributed by the Hancock Society, and in the next eleven months, another one hundred and fifty-five dollars were given. Thus, with the availability of people and money, the consolidation of land holdings and the erection of buildings for Believers and livestock dominated the decade.

The economic and industrial development occurring during this period was probably limited to the trades and activities carried on by the members before they joined. Those occupations needed to sustain a community set off from the rest of the world, such as blacksmithing, milling, and various aspects of farming, were undoubtedly practiced as well. An 1818 reference to the Hancock and New Lebanon Shakers states:

> . . . they also manufacture nearly all their own clothing and make many articles for sale, among which are leather, hats, cards, measures, boxes of beautiful workmanship, wire sieves, flax combs, waggons, plows, rails, wooden ware and brooms. They carry to market most kinds of kitchen vegetables; they also raise for sale abundance of garden seeds of every description common in these latitudes.

Those activities requiring special note during this time are the garden seed industry and broom making. While both began in communities other than Hancock, seed and broom shops were erected in four of the Hancock families — the West, Church, Second and East.

One serious setback befell the community as it entered the third decade of its existence. In the early spring of 1813, a fever swept through Hancock and the surrounding countryside. A letter from a sister at Hancock, dated April 13, states:

> On the 9th of Nov. Thomas Miller, Senior departed this life and on the 16th of Dec. Chloe Eddy was taken sick of a fever and died in about three days — since that time it has been very sickly here not one day has passed with less than 4 or 5 entirely confined and sometimes there has been from 12 to 15 sick at a time in the Church and many of them brought even to death's door.
> . . . It is not for the dead that we are distressed but for the living the dead are at peace but when it strikes at the vitals of the Church and tears out its strong foundation Pillars who shall protect the living.

It was noted that deaths were occurring so fast that in the case of Br. Willard and Br. Daniel Cogswell "they were both carried to the grave in the new burying yard north of the office and both put into one grave".

(left) Brother's felt hat
and dress coat

(bottom)
Mountain Meeting on Hancock's
Mt. Sinai, from David Lamson's
Two Years' Experience
Among the Shakers, 1848.

While this tragedy was immediately detrimental, it does not seem to have stopped the forward progress of the community. An 1818 visitor was particularly impressed with Hancock's water system and its use.

A small stream of water comes down from the mountains north of the town, near the source of which a dam is erected for the use of the thrashing mill. One man supplies the mill with sheaves; — it then falls into a fanning-mill, where the wheat is so completely separated that two men in eight hours can thrash and clean 80 bushels. Below this stands the corner grist-mill, and below that the saw-mill. From the saw-mill the stream is conducted by an aqueduct under ground to the middle of the village, where it is made to pass through a hollowed tree for the purpose of turning a large overshot wheel that serves to work their machinery. From this wheel the water is conveyed under ground to the washing rooms, and also for watering the horses, stables, works, & etc. . . . It also supplies the mill that saws firewood, pounds the wood that is split for basket making, and is afterwards conveyed to the different fields, to water the cattle & etc. Thus is everything under their control so directed that nothing is wasted.

On November 8, 1821, a North Family was established as part of the community at Hancock, located near the mills about three-quarters of a mile north of the Church Family, indicating that the numbers of members in the Church Family had increased to the point that another family was deemed necessary. This growth at the Church is further testified to by a schematic map of Hancock Church Family in 1820, probably the work of an elder or deacon in the family, showing a massive proliferation of dwellings, shops, and barns, some thirty-four in number.

Still, many buildings were described as barely adequate for various activities. The garden house was depicted, in 1821, as "far too small and cramped", as was the Tan House the following year. Soon older buildings began to be replaced by more substantial and up-to-date structures. When a fire in 1825 destroyed one of the earlier cattle barns of the Church, Elder William Deming, brother of Nathaniel Deming of the Hancock ministry, turned his engineering skills to the erection of the Round Stone Barn that was to replace the earlier structure. No other building, except possibly the 1830 Brick Dwelling House, would attest as well to the permanency with which the Shakers built during this period. Sparing no expense, the barn cost nearly $10,000, a sum thought to be ridiculous by the community's neighbors.

Meanwhile, other changes were taking place in the Society. In 1821, "The Millen-

Line Drawing of
Church Family 1961

Shaker apple corer

nial Laws or Gospel Statutes and Ordinances Adapted to the Day of Christ's Sec ond Appearing . . ." were adopted by the Church at New Lebanon and copied and read at Hancock within a few months. These laws, covering all facets of com munity life, provided a set of standards for all communities of the Shaker Society. Colors of buildings, furnishings of rooms, care of children, as well as rules of per sonal behavior, such as the crossing of the right hand over the left when sitting, were some of the subjects covered. About 1826, the use of alcohol or spirits within the Society was prohibited. In a letter to Father Job Bishop at Canterbury, New Hampshire, the ministry at Hancock noted: "We had the perusal of a letter which you sent to the Ministry of Lebanon . . . in which you manifested your feelings respecting the use of Spirits in which we fully unite, for we have made no use of spirits neither employed that mighty Doctor any way for 2 years . . ."

1826 Round Stone Barn after its reconstruction in 1864
(right) Earliest known Hancock seed packets

Village life in general settled into one of daily routine with thoughts of perfecting the communal lifestyle therein. In the early part of 1830, the Church Family began construction of their new dwelling house under the direction of Elder William Deming. This ultra-modern building with meeting room, dining hall and retiring rooms provided every convenience for the family. When the family moved in on the 22nd of November, 1831, there were 94 persons housed in it — 46 brethren and 48 sisters. The property of the community as a whole was approximately 2,000 acres by this time, and agricultural pursuits topped village activities. Large herds of Holstein dairy cattle grazed over the 800 or more acres serving as pastureland. Other lands saw the planting of crops of buckwheat, rye, oats, and hayseed. A postscript to an 1838 letter from the Hancock ministry reads: "The season here has been warm & vegetation exceeding luxuriant, grass and english grain perhaps never was better & also corn looks extremely well."

The garden seed industry continued to grow, and the preparation of dried green corn for sale soon ranked as a close second in the farm product line. Order blank seed lists, listing those "Garden Seeds Raised at Hancock, Berkshire County, Massachusetts And Neatly Put Up In Papers", saw sixty varieties advertised in 1829, and sixty-nine varieties in 1839.

The peddling of these seeds involved many brethren, who, like Joseph Patten and Phidelio Collins at the Church Family, spent many weeks traveling specific seed routes through New York and New England. Peddlers on the "Orange County Route" in 1849 collected $152.12 for seeds, and $48.37 for brooms, another product sold at the same time. The packets of seeds handled by the Shakers were sold on consignment to stores along the route. At the end of the summer, the seedsmen would call at the stores collecting the money for the seeds sold, giving the storekeepers their shares of the profits, and picking up all unsold seeds. Seeds from the previous season were never left on store shelves where they might spoil and jeopardize the Shaker reputation for quality.

From SHAKERS' GARDEN, Hancock, Massachusetts

LARGE WHITE MARROWFAT PEAS.

Plant as early as possible in light loamy soil, two inches deep, in double rows, nine inches apart, and three feet between the double rows. Bush five feet.

D. T.

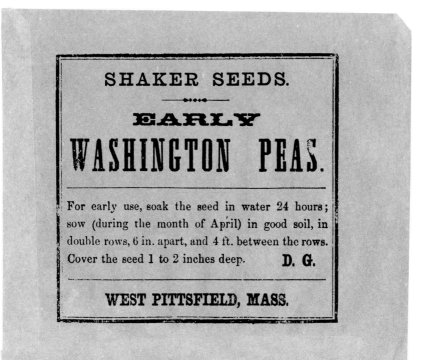

SHAKER SEEDS.

EARLY

WASHINGTON PEAS.

For early use, soak the seed in water 24 hours; sow (during the month of April) in good soil, in double rows, 6 in. apart, and 4 ft. between the rows. Cover the seed 1 to 2 inches deep. **D. G.**

WEST PITTSFIELD, MASS.

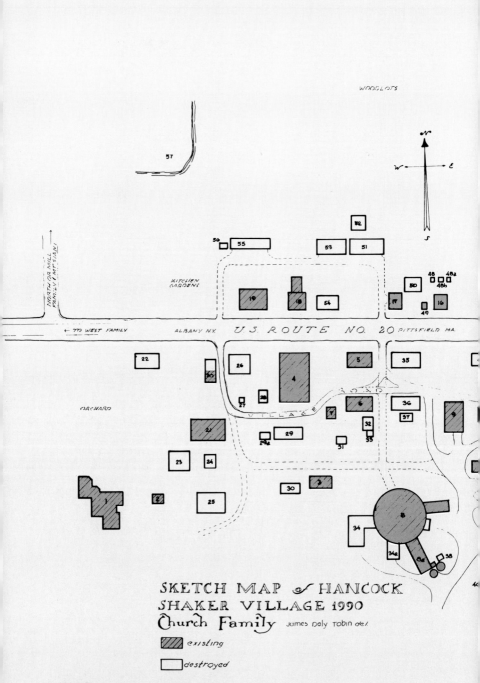

WOODLOTS

57

N
W ——— E
S

WEST FAMILY (MT. STA.)
NORTH OR MILL

52

56   55   53   51

KITCHEN
GARDENS

48 48a
50   48b
19   18   54   17   16
49

← TO WEST FAMILY   ALBANY N.Y.   U. S. ROUTE NO. 20 PITTSFIELD MA.

22   26   5   35

ORCHARD   56a
4   6   36
27   28   37   9
7
21   29   32
24a   33
23   24   51
30   3
2   25
1   8

34

34a

38

SKETCH MAP of HANCOCK
SHAKER VILLAGE 1990
Church Family James Daly Tobin del.

▨▨ existing

☐ destroyed

1985 Sketch map of the Church Family locating
all known and documented structures

1. Visitor Center 1972
2. Garden House
3. Poultry House 1878
4. Dwelling House 1830
5. Brethren Shop c. 1820
6. Sister Shop c. 1820
7. Ministry Wash House c. 1810
8. Round Stone Dairy Barn 1826
8a. Dairy Wing 1946
9. Barn c. 1820   Tan House 1835
10. Ice House 1894
11. Garage 1920
12. Deacon Shop c. 1815-1905   Garden
    Seed Shop moved to site Hired Men's 1905-1960
13. Horse & Hay Barn 1880 & 1910
13a. Cattle & Equipment Shed 1865
    Rebuilt 1968

13b. Dairy Wing 1939
14. Trustees' Office 1800 & 1895
14a. Office Privy
14b. Wagon & Grain Sheds
15. Cemetery 1813
16. School House c. 1815
17. Horse Barn 1850
18. Ministry Shop 1874-75
19. Meeting House 1786 Demolished
    1938-Shirley Meeting House 1792
20. Wood House (Sister Shop) 1868
    Garage 1914
21. Machine Shop & Laundry c. 1790-1875
22. Hatters' Shop c. 1800
23. First Dwelling House c. 1790
    Dry House 1830
24. Laundry Wood House c. 1840
25. Corn Drying House c. 1860
26. Sisters' Shop & Nurse Shop 1869
27. Ash House c. 1815
28. Summer House 1922
29. Woodhouse 1871
29a. Brethren Privy
30. Poultry Incubator c. 1870
31. Unidentified
32. Dairy Woodhouse
33. Sisters' Privy

TO EAST FAMILY NOVITIATE ⟶

34. Barn Ell (First Dairy Barn) c. 1800
34a. Barn Ell Unidentified
35. Boys' Shop c. 1840
36. Broom Shop c. 1825
37. Broom Shop Woodhouse
38. Milk House 1946
39. Slaughter House-Cider House
40. Corn Crib
41. Tin Shop c. 1820
42. Unidentified
43. Ash House
44. Tool House
45. Office Barn
46. Carriage Shed 1890
47. Blacksmith Shop c. 1790
48. Boys' Privy
48a. Girls' Privy
48b. Schoolhouse Woodshed
49. Tool Shed
50. Horse Stand
51. Lumber Shed
52. Unidentified
53. Lumber Shed
54. Garden Seed Shop c. 1800 moved 1905
55. Carriage Shed
56. Garden Tool Shed
57. Reservoir

III

The Peak Years

Among the many events taking place during the second quarter of the nineteenth century that affected the entire community was the development in each of the families of particular industrial or domestic activities. The Church Family was involved in the operation of mills; the first was a grist mill raised in 1823. An account of "The Expense of Bilding a Mill in 1823" notes:

Worke Done by the Church Brethren	2308 days
By the Sisters making bolts	22 Do
Teame worke with Oxen	355 Do
do do Horses	45 Do
The Other Expense by the Church	$2381.85

A Pittsfield chronicler states:

On the water privilege next below the factory built by Daniel Stearns in 1810, there was, in 1823, an old oil-mill; but in that year the privilege was bought by the Pittsfield and Hancock Shakers, who erected a dam and . . . a wooden grist mill, 40 feet by 30, two stories high, and containing two run of stones. The Shakers intended it for their own special convenience, but the excellence of their work soon gained it favor, which continued to increase until, in 1867, it was necessary to almost entirely rebuild it.

Sawmills were needed by the Shakers to produce the lumber for their many buildings and wood for their crafts. The Church, East, and Second Families each had one in operation. These were sometimes run by hired help; a journal from the Second Family notes: "Joseph Addams and Son come to commence tending mill tomorrow April 1, 1843 — our present Miller, Cyrus Worthy's time will then be out — sawed wood — water very scarce."

The last of the milling enterprises carried on at Hancock was carding and fulling. In 1845, the Church and East Families jointly erected a brick carding and fulling mill along Shaker brook near the North Family, between the grist and saw mills already operated by the Church.

Elder Henry Blinn described the mill in 1853: "It contains two double carding machines which have been in use for many years, also two looms and some other machinery. In case of failure of water, they have a small steam engine, which helps through the dry season." The operator and engineer of the woolen factory in 1856 was Richard Wilcox.

1876 map from Beers' Berkshire County Atlas
(below) Second Family Hancock c. 1875

Present Rte. 41 in foreground
Rte. U.S. 20 in background

Sophia Helfrich,
eldress, Second Family,
1835-1919

Hattie Emoretta Belden,
eldress and teacher, Church Family,
1862-1918

The factory did a thriving business during the 1850's and 60's, handling large amounts of cloth from the New Lebanon community as well as their own. In 1855, a receipt for "12 pieces of cloth to be Fulled and Dressed, 8 pieces of mixed, 4 pieces of butternut collor" was sent with Deacon Joseph Patten of Hancock to the mill. In the 1860 Berkshire County census, the woolen mill was listed as operating for three months and was valued at $4000. It employed eight people and had produced 766 yards of wool cloth, 650 yards of cotton cloth, and 300 pounds of wool yarn, all valued at $1472.

The diversification of commercial interests can be seen in the iron ore mines owned by and located on the East Family's lands. One report says the first iron ore mine was excavated before the year 1810 to a depth of sixty feet, with most of the ore going to the forges in Pittsfield. In later years, most of the iron was shipped to the furnace in Chatham, New York. Elder Henry Blinn commented on the mine in his journal:

> . . . a company has secured the rights to dig iron ore which is found in abundance. During the present season (1853) they have averaged about thirty tons a day. Some sixty men are employed at the mine. They have sunk a shaft some twelve feet in diameter and eighty feet deep. The ore is raised in buckets by horse power.

Ira R. Lawson,
trustee, and elder, Church Family,
1836-1905

Augustus Wells Williams,
elder, East Family
1805-1888

Rights to operate the mine were authorized or reauthorized periodically under fixed terms. In 1854, the trustees leased the rights to a Stephen R. Gay at "12½ per ton to Shakers for every ton over 2000 per year" for a period of five years. In later years, this would amount to about fifty dollars per ton, with a ton clearly specified at 2440 pounds. In a newspaper article in 1896, the profitability of the mine was noted:

> The Shakers certainly make a good thing of the mine. All they have to do is to keep their money bags open and let the shekels drop in. Their royalty up to the first of this month amounted to $500. a month or $6000. per year.

Another event of the first half of the nineteenth century was the coming of the railroad from West Stockbridge to Pittsfield and its passage over Shaker lands. In 1838, an agreement was reached between the trustees of the Hancock and Pittsfield Shaker Society and the Western Railroad Corporation for the sale of lands "for the track of their road to the extent in width authorized by this Charter." It called for the building of a bridge by the corporation to carry the highway over the tracks, several cattle cutouts, and drainage culverts, and a payment of $1620 for land, damages, and fencing. The Shakers may have had second thoughts about this seemingly lucrative agreement in the summer of 1839 when a ministry elder noted: ". . . arrived at Hancock 31st (August) found a number of brethren and sisters sick with a fever; caused as we thought by stagnant water, the common courses being stopped by the making of the Rail Road."

The first locomotive and car reached the Pittsfield Depot on May 4, 1841, and shortly thereafter, a station was built at the foot of the East Family, near to where the highway crossed the railroad. This is indicated by the fact that in 1844, the fifty-first post office established in Berkshire County was located at the station. In 1846, a visitor from Harvard records:

> . . . go to the East family nearest the depot . . . After dinner Elder Br. and myself with Br. Barnabas for conductor take a walk to the Depot . . . We went into the Depot looked around and were weighed. Shaker Village is over the door and West Pittsfield Post Office on the corner of the House.

The Shaker Village soon became one of the main attractions of a trip on the Western Railroad. An 1847 description of the route devotes an entire page to the Village, its people and their beliefs, and includes a woodcut of the Shaker crossing. To the Shakers, it proved to be an efficient means of travel for themselves and their friends, and an effective way to transport their products of industry.

While members of the United Society felt they could "say in truth, we receive no posts of honor, trust, or profit in the governments of this world," one exception was made in that of the office of postmaster or postmistress. In August 1854, Augustus W. William, elder of the East Family, was appointed postmaster and held the position until 1888. We can assume that the Society made this exception since the nearby post office would be handling primarily Shaker mail, and having a Believer in the office would be preferable to a person of the World. The town officials were undoubtedly pleased with the arrangement because of the Shaker reputation for scrupulous honesty.

Seeing themselves as God's children, the Shakers constantly practiced humility and Christian principles, setting nothing less than perfection as the goal in all facets of their lives. These values plus their desire to be anonymous parts of the Church's fellowship were manifested in the simplicity and practicality of their furniture, buildings, and artifacts and in the quality of their farm and commercial products. Their craftsmanship reached its high point in the Hancock community in the 1830's and '40's.

In the late 1830's, a new era swept in upon the Society known as the period of "Mother's Work." This era of mystical experience saw a new religious fervor take hold of the entire Shaker Society. Soon the leadership at New Lebanon felt the spiritual communications and manifestations being received by Believers might be a signal for a new dispensation or ordering of events. The growth of the Society and its material wealth seemed to indicate a movement away from the teachings of Mother Ann, and the time separating the current members from those who had known her represented a gap which called for a purging of the Society and a return to the strict following of her teachings and admonitions.

During 1838, the first spirit communications were received at Hancock and were soon being recorded by family instruments or visionists who were by definition those Believers capable of receiving and transmitting, either literally or pictorially, messages from the spirit world.

(right) Sewing stand with
two way drawer c. 1830

(below) Example of a basket
made by the Shakers

An 1843 introduction to a compilation of these messages states:

Through the goodness and mercy of God he has condescended to bless us with a revelation of his holy will. And through many chosen Instruments, we have received communications by which we have gained much knowledge respecting a spirit world, and the state of souls there in . . . The way and path of duty to us is plainly shown. Also the will of God is clearly now made known so that no one need murmur or say they do not know the way that heaven's treasures and gifts of God do flow.

Events began to occur in rapid succession. First on April 22, 1838, "the Church Family left the public meeting, and the families met by themselves for the first time." No longer was the public allowed to view the meetings of the Church. By divine inspiration, the name of Hancock was changed to "The City of Peace," and in 1841-2, every society was to prepare a place upon their highest piece of land for a "Holy place of worship" as pointed out by the prophets. At Hancock, on the mountain a half mile north of the settlement, an area called the "feastground" was cleared and named "Mount Sinai." The preparation for the spot was carried out through the joint efforts of all the families. On May 4, 1843, the fountain stone was erected upon which was engraved:

The Lord's Stone. Erected upon this Mt. Sinai May 4th, 1843 . . . And I command all people who shall come to this fountain, not to step within this enclosure, nor place their hands upon this Stone, while they are polluted with sin. I am God the Almighty in whose hands are judgement and mercy. And I will cause my judgements to fall upon the wilful violator of my commands in my own time according to wisdom and truth, whether in this world, or in eternity. For I have created all souls and unto me they are accountable. Fear Ye The Lord.

For the next ten or more years, the feastground was the site of some of the most unusual services held by the Society, including speaking in tongues, pantomime, and the visitation of spirits. Outsiders and new members who witnessed the services were called upon not to take lightly nor make fun of what they saw, for this was God's place and He was present to judge.

Hancock had an abundant number of mediums for receiving communications and transmitting them into written and pictorial form. Most famous of these was Sister Hannah Cohoon whose inspired drawings of various trees, such as 'The Tree Of Life', are examples of the Shakers' art.

The far-reaching aspects hoped for by the Society at this time are typified in a venture in which the ministry at Hancock took part — the distribution of the Sacred Roll. This book written by Philemon Stewart, a New Lebanon brother, defined the theology and new dispensation that meant the ultimate triumph of the sect in the World. On December 5, 1843, "Elder Grove W. Wright set out for Boston via Harvard, to carry the boxes of the Shaker Roll which is to go to all the Nations . . . Next morning commenced with our business in looking up the Consuls of different nations & disposing of the Books according to requirement, which took us till 3 o'clock PM on Saturday the 9th having had 40 books to dispose of." This included two copies each to the governors of Massachusetts and Rhode Island who happened to be in Boston that day.

(top) View of the center of the Church Family c. 1880
(bottom) Portrait of the Church Family sisters order c. 1890

(below) Church Family c. 1910.
(right) Wood casting pattern for Shaker line shaft pulley wheel
(overleaf) Eldress Sophia Helfrich and other Hancock Shakers
with friends at Niagara Falls c. 1893

IV

The Gradual Decline

In 1846, a Shaker compiled abstract of the population of the Hancock Community shows the following:

Family	Brethren	Sisters	Total
Church	35	50	85
Second	10	27	37
West	17	20	37
East	12	20	32
North	8	5	13
South	6	7	13
	88	129	217

This total membership of 217 was only exceeded in 1829 when there had been 116 brethren and 131 sisters for a total of 247 Believers. According to available research, this is the maximum population of the Hancock Society. By 1853, the population had dropped to 193 — 58 brethren and 135 sisters — a sharp decline of male membership.

During the period of the late 1840's and early 50's, the number of seceders from the Society was at a peak, but the decline from this point until 1960 was continual. An explanation for the sharp late 1840's drop can only be conjectured; in large measure it may have been the result of the operations and attitude of the Church during the period of Mother Ann's work. In trying to use this period of hyper-spiritualism to pull the Society more tightly together, the Church may have overstepped its bounds of credibility in both theology and practice. Some of the Believers found it impossible to kneel and bow down to Joseph Wicker and Simon Mabee as the instruments of God and Christ incarnate. As one seceder from this time states: "Who can believe that the Lord would come down from heaven and incarnate himself in a human being, make a formal address to an old man and not make him hear it! . . . It was not the Lord who spoke to us, but Jo Wicker."

*(top) 1867 Shaker grist and flour mill at Barkerville, W. Pittsfield, destroyed by fire in 1915
(bottom) Advertisement for Shaker mill products 1904*

Whatever the causes may have been, the drop in membership was a blow from which the Shaker Society would never fully recover. In 1849, the South Family, which had been established to handle the overflow of members from the Novitiate or East Family, was dissolved since there were too few new members to warrant two families.

As the mountain meetings and feastgrounds were abolished and the period of Mother Ann's work came to an end in the late 1850's, life in the community tended to settle down. Emphasis was once again placed on agriculture and domestic concerns. Visiting between selected members of the various communities became commonplace, with some sisters commenting on the amount of time they had to devote to the numerous visitors. In some cases, the journals from these visits provide the only description of a particular family's buildings and specific trades. On one visit by a group of Shakers from Enfield, Connecticut, in 1856, we get a glimpse of the West Family.

> . . . we found a very agreeable and loving little company, Marcia Boyington and Mary Ann Auger were the Eldresses. The family assembled together both brethren and sisters; we visited sung and danced had a refreshing time out that we walked about some, to the wash house, cheese house, sisters shop, a very pleasant situation, we then traveled back to the dwelling house where we ate our supper which they had so nicely prepared for us . . .

At least one business activity occurred at this time in the West Family. David Terry, elder of the family, made an agreement with John Low of Bridgeport, Connecticut, in which Low, for the sum of one dollar, acquired the twenty year rights "to dig for mines and minerals my Cook lot (so called) situated in said Hancock. Said Low is to make his examination and do all the work at his expense, and to give said Terry one tenth percent of the minerals found and dug out." No later mention appears on the outcome of this venture, but its possible long-range benefits typify the kind of agreement the Shakers always tried to arrange.

In all the families of the community, the gradual decreasing membership was felt, and in an attempt to counter this drop in the work force, numerous apprenticeship agreements were entered into between the Shakers and the World. The Believers offered to train boys and girls, men and women, in some trade or occupation with all the benefits of family membership, such as care during illness, clothing, and clean and comfortable living quarters, in exchange for their time and services for the use and benefit of the particular family.

The outbreak of the Civil War in 1860 and the resultant abolition of practically all the military exemption laws dealt a serious blow to the Society as a whole. For more than sixty years the Shakers had struggled to establish military exemption laws based on their religious beliefs. This process had involved court cases, jailings, scores of newspaper articles, and the publication of a full discussion of their total commitment to pacifism.

For the next three years, brethren in all the villages were forced to appear before conscription boards in various cities to be examined and classified for possible duty. In an effort to effect a change of this practice, both a written appeal and a personal visit were made to President Lincoln and Secretary of War Stanton by Frederick Evans and Benjamin Gates on behalf of the entire society.

(left) Three slat side chair
with "listing" or tape seat

(below) Detail of button tilter
used to prevent wear
on floors and rugs

(overleaf) Examples of turned
Shaker pegs and drawer pulls

Trustees' Office and Store in the 1880's

The matter came down to a question of dollars and cents. Because the Society forbade its members from drawing pensions and bounty lands from the federal government for past military services, the Society members were owed over $600,000 for services rendered before they had joined. Elder Evans pointed out that the maximum amount of money the government could receive for military substitutes or fines levied against the roughly seventy eligible brethren was no more than $28,200; so he suggested that these brethren be exempted from duty in exchange for the Society's promise to abstain from drawing on the $600,000 from the already overburdened federal treasury. His plan was adopted in substance, although not in form; the result was that all the eligible brethren were drafted but put on indefinite furlough.

In 1867, Secretary Stanton visited Mount Lebanon and, referring to the matter said:

I understood the case, and after consulting the President, we acted according to your desire, and I have always been thankful that I could in any way befriend you. I hope your society will always prosper, that God's blessing may rest upon it and that you who have joined hands may be reunited in the spirit land.

In 1867, upon the death of Elder David Terry, the decision was made by Elder Grove Wright of the ministry to dissolve the West Family, and on November 25th the family was broken up. Shortly thereafter the same fate befell the North Family; it was closed and its dwelling house was moved to the Church Family to replace a sisters' shop which had burned the year before. The North Family closing seems

Trustees' Office and Store after its Victorianization in 1895

to have been precipitated by an 1865 fire which destroyed the valuable carding and fulling mill.

Fire was a problem that caused the Hancock Shakers, especially the Church Family, a great deal of time, money and concern. Previous to the two fires mentioned above, the Round Stone Barn had burned on December 1, 1864, set off by the careless handling of a lantern. Its loss was estimated at $15,000. Four years later, the fire which destroyed the Sisters' Shop and a Nurse Shop was listed as a loss of not less than $7,000. Together these losses represent a staggering sum of money, especially since the substantial revenue from the carding mill was lost as well.

As always the elders and eldresses kept up the spirits of the family with repeated words of encouragement and the positive belief that God was at work in His many and complex ways. As the Society moved into the 1870's, it continued to manifest a look of health and prosperity.

In the September 1872 issue of the Society's own publication, "The Shaker," editor George Lomas noted:

> Passing through Hancock recently, we were pleasantly surprised at her improved appearance. Always neat, she now looks beautiful. Meeting house modernized; the antiquated, elevated aqueduct by the roadside is no more; beautiful stone fences, with posts and boards above; large permanent gates, painted red, and fastened by spring padlocks — all looking rejuvenated. Very likely her people are being illustrated as those consecrated souls who 'put their hands to work, and give their hearts to God.'

Although by now only three families with 98 members remained, Hancock still had many good years ahead. In agricultural pursuits alone, nearly a thousand acres were under cultivation and farm machinery was valued at $31,000. Indian corn, oats, barley, and wheat constituted the major crops with potatoes and orchard products listed as other staples of the farm. Other agricultural industries, such as the garden seed industry and the growing of sage, had dropped off drastically after the Civil War. In 1864, the gross receipts from the seed industry had fallen to $2,922.54, a drop of almost $4,000 since 1850, and the income from seeds, brooms, and sage together only amounted to $2,525 in 1874.

Brother Ira Lawson who was one of the trustees of the Church Family at this time had been a farm deacon for years and had a keen business sense that was unequalled at Hancock. Under his guidance, the Church began to raise and breed cattle for area markets.

It was also under Ira Lawson's leadership that the Church Family's grist mill in West Pittsfield was rebuilt in 1867. It was described as three full runs of stone, ''one of which is devoted entirely to the grinding of wheat''. The mill was of great service and convenience to the people of the surrounding community for forty-eight years until 1915, when it was destroyed by fire.

The vast amount of land which the Shakers owned proved to be a problem as the membership and vitality of the community decreased. As each Shaker family closed, lands were consolidated, and throughout the 1870's and 1880's, the Church, Second and East Families shuffled parcels of land back and forth in an attempt to firm up their property boundaries. On a Hancock property survey map of 1887, the community owned six major parcels of land totaling 2,817½ acres. By 1901, the Society's land problems had become so acute that an advertisement placed in a Pittsfield paper announced: ''2,500 acres for Sale — in West Pittsfield — Sold by Ira Lawson Trustee and Thomas N. Enright — sold so people could build country houses''.

A last land venture that would prove financially disastrous involved the closing of the Tyringham Shaker community in 1875. On January 1, 1876, the Ministry at Lebanon traded the Tyringham property which had been valued at $25,000, plus other Shaker lands in Wisconsin, Michigan, and New York for a 10,000 acre timber lot in Pennsylvania valued at $120,000. The New Lebanon community borrowed $30,000 from Hancock toward the deal and signed over half of the property to the Hancock Church Family. In 1904, Hancock was able to recover $5,000 by the sale of their interest to the North Family, Mount Lebanon Shakers; in 1905 the entire timber lot was sold to the State of Pennsylvania for $13,000.

Overall, however, Shaker life in the last quarter of the nineteenth century was routine and peaceful in nature. Some commentators felt it was too peaceful: ''In the settlement itself an eternal Sabbath seems to reign; all is so silent and lifeless that one involuntarily thinks of a Deserted Village with the inhabitants just gone and everything left in 'apple-pie' order.'' Life in the community went on; new buildings were erected. For the first time plantings of trees, shrubs, and flowers were done for the sake of ornamentation as well as their practical uses. A new Ministry Shop was erected in 1873-74 and a brick Poultry House in 1878; a new brick Ice House followed in 1894. Other structures were brought up to date, such as the Trustees' House, which was modernized to a high Victorian appearance.

(above) Visitors on front porch of Trustees Office c. 1905

(right) Copy of Table Monitor from the Visitors' Dining Room

TABLE MONITOR.

GATHER UP THE FRAGMENTS THAT REMAIN, THAT NOTHING BE LOST.—Christ.

Here then is the pattern
  Which Jesus has set;
And his good example
  We cannot forget:
With thanks for his blessings
  His word we'll obey;
But on this occasion
  We've somewhat to say.

We wish to speak plainly
  And use no deceit;
We like to see fragments
  Left wholesome and neat:
To customs and fashions
  We make no pretence;
Yet think we can tell
  What belongs to good sense.

What we deem good order,
  We're willing to state—
Eat hearty and decent,
  And clear out our plate—
Be thankful to Heaven
  For what we receive,
And not make a mixture
  Or compound to leave.

We find of those bounties
  Which heaven doth give,
That some live to eat,
  And, that some eat to live—
That some think of nothing
  But pleasing the taste,
And care very little
  How much they do waste.

Tho' Heaven has bless'd us
  With plenty of food:
Bread, butter and honey
  And all that is good;
We lothe to see mixtures
  Where gentle folks dine,
Which scarcely look fit
  For the poultry or swine.

We find often left,
  On the same china dish,
Meat, applesauce, pickle,
  Brown bread and minc'd fish;
Another's replenish'd
  With butter and cheese;
With pie, cake and toast,
  Perhaps, added to these.

Now if any virtue
  In this can be shown,
By peasant, by lawyer,
  Or king on the throne,
We freely will forfeit
  Whatever we've said,
And call it a virtue
  To waste meat and bread.

Let none be offended
  At what we here say;
We candidly ask you,
  Is that the best way?
If not,—lay such customs
  And fashions aside,
And take this monitor
  Henceforth for your guide.

Shaker Home, 1830

[VISITOR'S DINING ROOM, SHAKER VILLAGE.]

Many of these changes were a result of the new leadership of the Society; the old-line elders had passed on, and men like Elder Frederick Evans of Mt. Lebanon urged change and updating of the communities in both physical appearance and theological doctrine. Much of the physical improvement seems to have been done in an attempt to encourage young Believers to remain and outsiders to join.

The Church and its remaining two families continued to produce various wares such as brooms, tubs, pails, and swifts. In addition, garden seeds, applesauce, and a particular type of Hancock chair were produced for sale to visitors.

On the death of Elder Thomas Damon of the Hancock ministry in 1880, Elder Albert Battles, formerly head of the Tyringham Community, succeeded to the office. He and Caroline Helfrich were the last ministry at Hancock. On June 18, 1893, word came from the New Lebanon ministry that the bishopric at Hancock was abolished and that direct rule would be exerted by New Lebanon. Albert Battles became a trustee with Ira Lawson; Carolyn Helfrich was made elder sister in the family.

Hired men had now become an institution on the Shaker farm, providing the necessary manpower to keep it operating. In 1874, about twenty-five men were employed by the Church. Buildings were moved and converted for their use and in some cases even for their families.

The advent of the twentieth century forecast little hope of a rebirth of the Shaker movement. The family welcomed the arrival of rural free mail delivery in 1903 and the purchase of their first automobiles a few years later. On August 19, 1911, however, the East Family was finally dissolved and its buildings and land sold to diverse parties. The family journals continued to record the loss of members to the world and fires once again claimed many structures, such as the Deacons' Shop in 1905 and the Brethren's Shop of the Second Family the same year. In 1910, the Calf Barn at the Church and in 1915 the West Pittsfield Grist Mill were added to this list. By 1903, the use of the Meeting House and dancing services had been discontinued. The Shaker Schoolhouse was down to its last few students and, in 1934, was sold after more than a hundred years of use. The old "furnace property" with its iron mines, which had closed at the turn of the century, was sold in 1921 for a mere $1,600. Even the capable Elder and Trustee Joseph Holden, appointed at the death of Ira Lawson in 1905, and his successor, Sister Frances Hall, appointed in 1919, were able only to stem, but not reverse, the continual pattern of decline.

An article on the Shakers in 1934 remarks:

> . . . there are flowers and shrubs, climbing vines and graceful arbors; and the rustic flagstone walks lend their attraction.
> Nevertheless, there is a prevailing sense of encroaching delapidation, fences are allowed to get decrepit, and the less important buildings are being worsted in the warfare with nature. But what else could be expected? Only twenty-five members are there now — not enough to keep the place going — and all except two are women.

Sister Anna Delcheff in hooded cape c. 1928

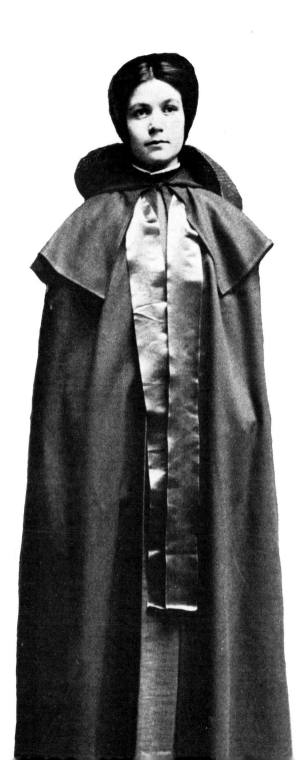

Former sister Olive Hayden, during a recent interview, provided a picture of life within the family before her apostacy in 1935. As a young girl, her life at Hancock had been busy but relatively carefree. She still remembers playing with several other young girls in the Brethren's Shop, in a room where the sisters then lined sewing boxes being made for sale. By 1930, most of her contemporaries had left, and she felt extremely burdened by having to care for so many aging sisters. When word came that the community at New Lebanon might move to Hancock with another group of elderly sisters, she knew she could no longer stay. In 1935, at the urging of her brother, a non-Shaker, she left her home of thirty-two years and entered the alien world.

Finally, early in 1948, the headquarters of the United Society at Mt. Lebanon, New York, was closed and the remaining members moved to Hancock. Here under Eldress Fannie Estabrook, the family carried on until 1960. These last years saw many of the best known buildings demolished, such as the Meeting House in 1938 and, in 1958, the long-patronized Shaker Store where candy and knit goods had been sold to visitors for years. Also in 1958, Ricardo Belden, the last brother at Hancock, died.

Since there were only three aged sisters left, the Central Ministry at Canterbury, New Hampshire, decided to close the community. In 1959, the land and buildings were offered for sale, and a group of local citizens formed to try to acquire the site as an outdoor museum to interpret the Shaker way of life and to preserve the remaining buildings. On October 15, 1960, the property, consisting of 900 acres and 17 buildings, was sold to a group soon to be known as Shaker Community, Inc., for $125,000 and the restoration of Hancock Shaker Village began.

Eldress Fannie Estabrook, last Hancock Eldress, c. 1958

*Four Samuel Chamberlain
views of the Church Family
in the late 1950's*

1

Visitors' Center

This modern facility, erected in 1972, was designed along contemporary lines and offers the necessary services for the many thousands of visitors who call at Hancock Shaker Village each year. Erected outside the limits of the historical village, the building was felt to best represent many of the design elements of the Shaker buildings in the museum complex. With its spacious open areas, exposed pine frame, and original use of natural light, it captures the feeling of a building that might have been erected here by the Shakers themselves if the Hancock community still flourished.

The ticket and information desk, a museum store and bookshop, lunch shop, restrooms and the Village's Business Offices are located here. In the main entry hall are changing exhibits about the Shaker community at Hancock from its founding in 1790 to the present.

Surrounding the Visitors' Center and its adjacent parking area is the 'Tree of Life Arboretum.' Begun in 1972, the Arboretum is composed of the trees and shrubs grown and enjoyed by the Hancock Shakers, following the precedent set by Elder Henry Blinn who established an arboretum at the Shaker Village in Canterbury, New Hampshire, in the late nineteenth century. Donors have given the trees in honor of and in memory of friends and relatives; anyone interested in helping with this important environmental project is invited to contact the Village office.

(left) Visitors' Lunch Shop
(bottom) Visitors' Center and Village Offices

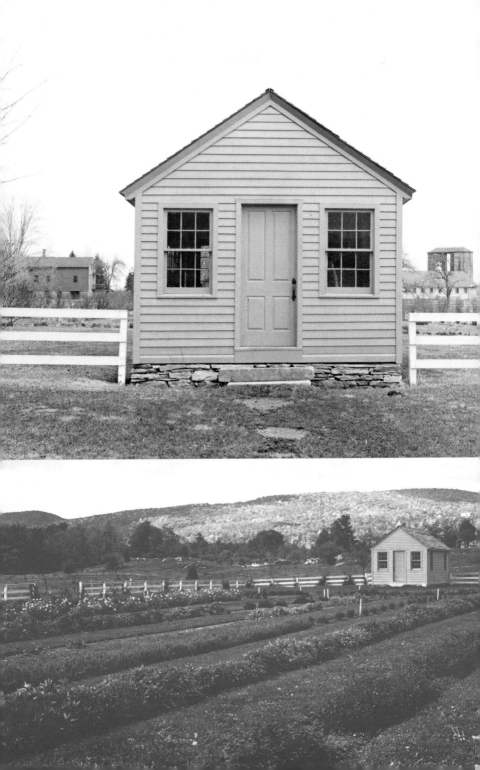

2

Garden Tool Shed and Herb Garden

This small structure was originally built as a summer house in 1922 near the main brick dwelling as a place for the Shaker sisters to enjoy the warm, balmy evenings of the summer and fall and to have tea in the late afternoon.

In 1961, as the area around the main dwelling house was being restored to the period of the 1840's, the building was moved and rebuilt as a Garden Tool Shed. It was placed on the foundation of a tool shed which had been adjacent to the large brick corn drying house erected by the Society in the late 1850's to house this important farm industry, which flourished until the turn of the twentieth century. Sometime during the 1930's, the corn house was demolished as a tax and insurance liability.

Since there were no plans to rebuild the corn drying house, the designation of the summer house as the Garden Tool Shed was felt appropriate, as Hancock was soon to install an Herb Garden to the east of the building, and a place was needed to interpret their gardening practices.

The Herb Garden contains medicinal and culinary herbs raised by the United Society for sale to the "World" and for use by their own physicians in making extracts and medicinal preparations. The rose bushes lining the runs of white fences are "Rosa Gallica Officinalis". The roses were raised solely from their functional value; the petals were dried and prepared as an extract to make the famous Shaker Rosewater which was used as a flavoring for apple pies and as a soothing wash to bathe the sick. The fruit or hips were used to make Rose Hip Jelly, a specialty of the Shaker kitchen sisters.

(left) Garden Tool Shed
(lower left) Village Herb Garden
(below) Shaker side hill plow with wrought iron plowshare c. 1800

3

Poultry House

The raising and breeding of poultry had been underway at Hancock since early in the nineteenth century. Poultry and hen houses are shown on almost every known map of the Hancock community. The expertise of the Church Family was noted in 1846 by a visiting brother: "Before breakfast I went out to the Elders shop conversed with Br. Joseph on the management of poultry — saw a new work on that subject by C. Bement." The Church Family sold eggs for years, and many local people remember calling at the Brick Dwelling House for their purchase.

The fact that the building is constructed of brick attests to the value placed by the family on their flocks. With the often severe New England winters, the warmth and protection of these important animals were given a high priority. The east end of the first floor was used as a calving pen, with hay stored in the attic loft. A stove with its chimney allowed feed to be heated.

During the museum's first years of operation, this structure, which had fallen into disrepair, was restored and adapted in 1964 to house a museum store, gallery areas, and the Village offices. With the opening of the new Visitors' Center in 1972, it was converted to gallery use on the first floor, and the Village library on the second.

Among the highlights of Hancock Shaker Village's collections are twenty-four rare Shaker spirit or "gift" drawings. These watercolors were created in the 1840s and 1850s by Shakers who received visions and messages from angels and spirits. The drawings were not intended for decoration, but to record and share deeply spiritual experiences.

The research library on the second floor houses the Village's collections of Shaker publications, photographs, manuscripts, ephemera, and material written about the Shakers. The library is open to the public for research by appointment.

(top) Brick Poultry House now Village library and orientation center
(bottom) Sister Jennie Petiff with her flock of white leghorns, 1925.

(below) The Tree of Life, seen and painted by Sister Hannah Cohoon, Hancock, 1854
(right) A Little Basket Full of Apples, Hannah Cohoon, 1856
(overleaf) Present from Mother Lucy to Eliza Ann Taylor, New Lebanon, N.Y. 1849

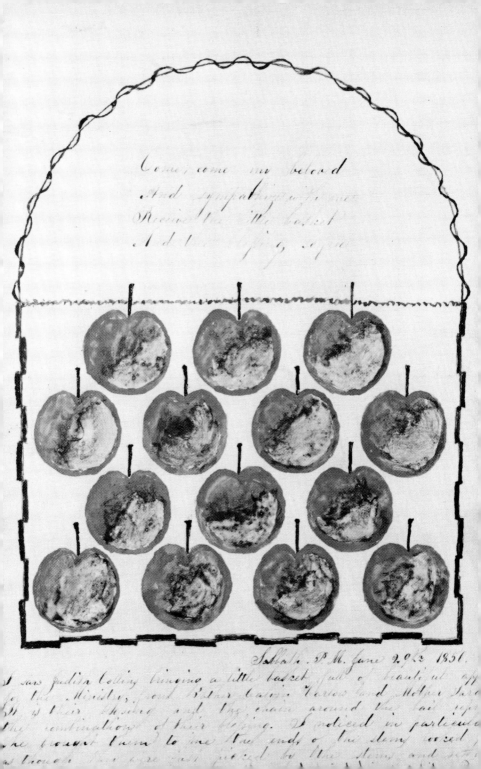

Brick Dwelling House

One of the most impressive structures within the Church Family, the Brick Dwelling House was erected in 1830 to house nearly one hundred Believers. Raised to accommodate the growing population of the family, it replaced a smaller structure which stood to the west of the present dwelling and burned in 1868.

The handsomely appointed building was designed and executed by Elder William Deming who, in January 1832, wrote to Elder Benjamin Youngs:

And as to myself in addition to all my common concerns, I have headed and assisted in the building of the whole house, in both the mason and joiner work.

He provides a complete account of the erection of the building and descriptions of the many unique features of it.

We began laying the foundation on the 15th of April 1830 with the materials as follows: 2,326 feet of white hewn stone 30 cts. per foot — this includes the underpinning, belting, Window caps and sils with the watertable and door posts. In addition to this 565 feet of blue limestone that we sawed and cut ourselves for the basement story at the south end of the house — which forms the outside walls of the cook room. Also 330 feet of blue limestone sawed six inches thick with the sawed edges out, this is placed under the underpinning. Now add 350 thousand brick with these materials and stone for the cellar walls; we commenced our building and in ten (10) weeks from the placing of the first stone in the cellar, the house was neatly laid up and the roof put on . . . The work is all well done. There is none to excel it in this country. And the same can be said of the joiner work — the stuff is very clear; scarcely a knot can be seen in all the work, except for the floors and they are yellow pine and very good. There are 100 large doors including outside and closet doors; 245 Cupboard doors — 369 drawers — These we placed in the corners of the rooms and by the sides of the chimneys. The drawers are faced with butternut and handsomely stained — they take

(top) 1830 Brick Dwelling House. Chief architect Elder William Deming
(left center) Main bake oven and flanking arch kettles for cooking vegetables
(right center) Believers' Dining Room
(lower left) North wall of Sisters' Retiring Room
(lower right) First floor plan showing primary communal rooms

up but little room, and are not to be cleaned under. Next there are 95 24 lighted windows . . . In all 3,194 squares of glass including inside and out. The Meeting room is on the North end of the house and is 50 by 22 with two partitions which forms the hall. Part of which swings back & shuts across the hall, and the other part runs up between the upper walls so that the floor is a smooth space without any threshold. The dining room is at the South end with accommodations for 80 persons to sit down at one time. The victuals is conveyed up into the dining room by means of two sliding cupboards. The Ministry has a neat little dining room adjoining the large one. The cook room is very convenient; we have excellent water from a never failing spring that is conveyed into the cook room in three different places and two places in the second loft. There is two excellent ovens made on an improved plan which will bake four different settings at one heating. Also the arch kettles are on a new plan of my own invention, and which proves to be the best ever seen about here . . . And I think we may say it is finished from the top to the bottom, handsomely stained inside with a bright orange color. The out doors are green. The outside of the house is painted with four coats of a beautiful red. The plastering is covered with a coat of hard finish & is a beautiful white . . . Now Elder Benjamin I suppose you will think — I wonder what the expenses of all this might be. Well this is rather hard to come at but I will try to give you a little idea. We have found all the materials ourselves — such as sand, lime, stone & etc. with all the timber except the flooring. Made all the windows, doors, cupboards and drawers, hung them and put on the trimmings . . . With all this and a great deal more that we have done ourselves, the out expenses are about 8,000 dollars. The whole work has been performed in the space of nineteen months . . . Now Elder Benjamin I think by the time you have read all my broken scrawl you will think our purse is pretty empty, which in truth is the case. But as we have received in obedience to our good Mother Ann's words — So we expect to receive. Her precious words were these, "Your hands to work and your hearts to God and a blessing will attend you." This we have found true.

When the family moved into their new house on November 22, 1831, there were 94 people housed within — 46 brethren and 48 sisters. From that time until 1960 when the Village closed, this building was the focal point of communal life; eating, sleeping, and daily worship all took place within its walls.

Another room on the basement level of special note is the buttery or as we refer to it today, the "Good Room." Originally the "Good Room," the first open room on the right after the center hall axis, was used for the best jams, jellies, pickles, and other preserved foods the Shaker sisters had to offer. Today the Good Room, staffed largely by volunteers, offers for sale these same types of foodstuffs, along with various baked goods made from Shaker recipes.

The allocation of space within the Brick Dwelling House remained generally the

(top) Second attic loft and flying staircase
(bottom) Axis of second floor halls with sisters'
staircase on the left and brethren's on the right

same throughout the years of Shaker occupancy. The basement was devoted to the kitchens and dairy rooms with the remaining areas for wet and dry storage of staples, meats, and preserves.

On the first floor at opposite ends were the primary communal rooms — the dining room where the Shaker brethren and sisters ate their meals in silence at 6 a.m., 12 noon and 6 p.m., and the meeting room where both singing and labouring services were held at 8 p.m. in the evening. The other rooms on this floor were used as waiting rooms for the members before meals — a time of gathering, prayer, and meditation and as retiring rooms for the elders and eldresses.

The numbers over the doors were used by the deacons to list the pieces of furniture assigned to each room and to maintain a record of the family members who lived in each.

The second and third floors of the house were used as "retiring" or sleeping rooms, where from two to four members would reside, brethren on the east and sisters on the west, each sex with a separate stairway and entrance door. Today three of the rooms are shown as retiring rooms; the rest interpret occupations, quarters, or activities which took place in buildings no longer extant at the Village. Interpretive labels define or explain the setting.

The third floor, closed to the public due to state fire laws, houses the offices of the museum's curatorial, interpretive, and education departments.

The two attic lofts, also closed to the public, were used by the Shakers for storage areas and occasionally as retiring rooms.

(above) Second floor hallway
with doorways to brethren
and sisters retiring rooms

(left) One of the twenty
built-in cupboard-drawer
storage systems

(below) Hancock
commode vented directly
into the chimney
to eliminate odor

5

Brethren's Shop

I N accordance with the Gospel order that the sexes have separate work places to carry out their crafts or industries, the two and one-half story Brethren's Shop was raised in the late 1790's.

Here until the death of Brother Ricardo Belden in 1958, the Shaker brothers carried on a variety of small manufactures and trades in shops like this one designed specifically for their hand labor. Trades practiced by these men in this type of shop in various communities might have included, coopering, tinsmithing, broom and brush making, oval and round box making, clockmaking, harness making, shoe making, chair and cabinetmaking, button making, or the manufacture of yarn swifts for winding yarn, wire toothed cards for carding wool, spinning wheels and reels, and smoking pipes and stems. A variety of these trades is presently demonstrated or exhibited in the Brethren's Shop.

This shop, which was partially restored in 1962-63, is only one of several Brethren's Shops once found in the family not including the machine shops, tannery, hatters shop, male nurse shop and lesser structures which were principally reserved for the male members of the sect. Additional restoration in 1973 involved excavating portions of the basement; during this work several stone-cutting tools and many stone chips were found, leading to the assumption that the engraving of headstones for the nearby cemetery was done in this building.

Broom making was one of the major trades carried on at Hancock. In 1860, three families had broom shops with capital invested of $1090, including thirteen tons of broom corn, and production for the year of 16,500 brooms worth $2,934.

The Shakers had a firm belief in the value of work. A contemporary account of the Shakers states:

> Every man among the brethren has a trade, some of them have two, even three or four trades. No one may be an idler, not even under the pretence of study, thought and contemplation. Everyone must take his part in family business; it may be farming, building, gardening, smith work, painting, everyone must follow his occupation, however high his calling or rank in the church . . . The Shakers believe in variety of labor, for variety of occupation is a source of pleasure, and pleasure is the portion meted out by an indulgent Father to his saints.

A description of the inhabitants of one shop was given by another visitor: "We found a number of men at work — all of them with the same tranquil and subdued expression. No excitement, no friction, no competition enter these abodes of fellowship and peace."

(top) Brethren's Shop with carriage landing
(bottom) Winder used in the manufacture of Shaker brooms

Products and views of the Brethren Shop. Brother Ricardo Belden, at center, was the last Hancock brother to occupy the shop.

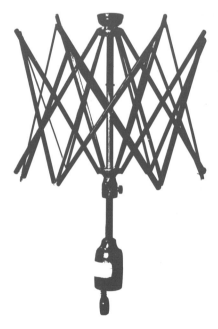

6

Sisters' Dairy
and Weave Shop

The Shakers tended dairy herds soon after the community's founding, and by 1795, the Sisters' Dairy was established on this site. In 1816, it was noted that the three buildings then devoted to the dairy industry were inadequate, due to the success of their dairy activities. To assure the safe keeping of milk, the Shakers put in cooling tanks with continuously flowing water shortly after 1880. Elder Louis Basting installed electric churns in the 1930's, and former sister Olive Hayden remembers spending long hours running the churns and working the butter. The building remained in use until the 1940's.

The Sisters' Dairy was enlarged after 1820 to house another activity. The building was raised an entire story and a two-room weaving loft was added where the sisters could busy themselves while waiting for the milk to arrive from the barns. Frame looms, tape looms, wool and flax wheels were all used to produce whole cloth and linen. The constant demand for these fabrics which were needed by the ever growing family kept the shuttles flying. The need for cloaks, sheets, clothing, blankets, rugs, and chair tapes seemed endless; so new pieces of machinery were constantly being introduced to help with the many tasks. An 1849 journal notes:

> Henry DeWitt came over from Lebanon to bring a Pleasant Spinner. Sister Eliza Ann came to assist in putting it in order and show the sisters how to use it. Maria Lapsla came to learn the English manner of combing worsted.

As the family grew and the industrial activities of the sisters became more complex, other structures were raised to meet the specialized needs of both brethren and sisters, such as clothier shops, seed shops, and nurse shops. Other shops were built which were devoted solely to occupations of the female line such as the preparation and packaging of medicines, the drying of green sweet corn, the manufacture of sewing notions and boxes. The journal of a Hancock sister noted her work for the months of April, May and June, 1863:

(top) Sisters' Shop with dyeing frame in foreground.
(bottom left) Hancock table swift for winding skeins of yarn into balls for knitting
(bottom right) Shaker screw type cheese press

(above left) Shaker clock reel

(above) Hands of a Hancock sister
weaving a rag rug c. 1935

(left) Butter churn

(right) Four harness loom from
the Shaker Community
Enfield, Connecticut

Commenced making butter and cheese
Butter made in 1863 (totaled 875 lbs.)
Cut and mad 25 coats & trousers
Wove 25 doz. bonnets
Finished spinning the carpet yarn
Knitted 9 par socks — footed 9 par socks
Cut and made 2 dresses, made & mended little things
Looked over 100 wts. of palm

The main sisters' shop at the Church Family, which was razed in 1958, housed the manufacture of baskets, sewing boxes and candy, and stood just to the west of the main dwelling.

The privy behind the Sisters' Shop was built in the 1840s by the South Family at the Shaker village in Harvard, Massachusetts. It was moved to the village in 1990 and stands on the site of the original Sisters' Shop privy.

7

Ministry Wash House

One of the smallest buildings within the confines of the Church Family, this building was used by the members of the Hancock ministry and visiting ministries for washing their clothes and bathing.

Wash houses of various types are often mentioned in journals of visitors to the Family. In 1846, a member of the Harvard ministry noted:

> This morning for the first time since I left home I arise and immediately go to the bath house a small brick building near the machine shop built exclusively for bathing.

The stove used to heat this building is one of the earliest varieties of Shaker plate stoves. Developed along the lines of the Franklin stove, it has a wide ash shelf and hinged front face which acts as a single large damper.

The Ministry Wash House and interior furnishings

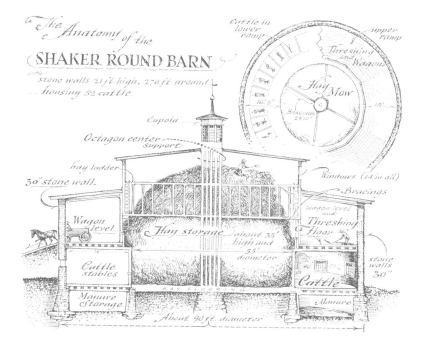

The Anatomy of the

SHAKER ROUND BARN

with stone walls 21 ft. high, 270 ft. around, housing 52 cattle.

Cattle in lower ramp

upper ramp

Threshing and Wagons

Hay Mow

16.3"

BRACINGS 23'10"

15'

Cupola

Octagon center support

hay ladder

30" stone wall.

Windows (14 in all)

Bracings

wagon level and Threshing Floor

Wagon level

Hay storage *about 35' high and 55' diameter*

Cattle stables

Manure Storage

HAY FLOORING

Cattle

stone walls 30"

Manure

About 90 ft. diameter

8

Round Stone Barn

Of all the buildings erected by the United Society, none has attracted more attention than the Round Stone Barn built in 1826. Built to replace an earlier cattle barn which had burned in 1825, the barn was raised with the help of hired masons who were paid $500 and boarded. What prompted the building of a round barn will probably never be known since only scanty documentation exists.

An 1829 account of the building describes its physical features:

It is 270 feet in compass, with walls laid in the line rising 21 feet above the underpinning, and from 3½ to 2½ feet in thickness. The masts and rafters are 53 feet in length and united together at the top. On the lower floor, immediately within the walls, are stables 8 feet high, occupying 12 feet in length with the manger which is inwards and into which convenient places are left for throwing hay and feed from above. In these stables which open to and from several yards, a span of horses and 52 horned cattle may be stabled. The covering of the stables forms the barn floor, onto which from an offset there is but one large door for teams, which make the circut of the floor and pass out at the same place. Eight or 10 can occupy the floor at the same time; and the hay is thrown into the large area at the center.

The interior arrangement of the barn was probably altered as the Shakers replaced their "horned," that is longhorned cattle, with the new breeds of milking shorthorns. The shorthorns would have allowed the Shakers to fit more cattle in the same space. A drawing, published in an agricultural newspaper, of the barn's floor plan in 1857, shows stalls for 70 cattle and calving pens.

The barn, with its conical roof, made an impression on every visitor, Shaker and non-Shaker alike. Sister Lucy Hammond noted; "Went to see the Round Stone Barn; it is a very curious and singular constructed building, there is a flight of stairs in the inside to go up and down."

On December 1, 1864, fire struck the barn and the loss was estimated at $15,000 including wagons, a hundred tons of hay and farm equipment.

The barn was rebuilt the next year with a flat roof topped by a cupola to replace the conical roof. In the mid-1870's the last addition to the barn was made — the monitor, or twelve-sided superstructure, was added to the roof to provide ventilation and increased headroom for brothers at haying time.

(top) Round Stone Barn with dairy wing and twin silos, c. 1935.
(bottom) Barn elevation by Eric Sloane for An Age of Barns, 1966

The building of the manure pit in 1880 undermined the stability of the barn's massive stone walls, resulting in cracking which threatened the building with collapse. In 1968, the barn and its brick ell were finally restored to their earlier appearance.

Today the barn stands as an architectural monument and as a prime example of the Shakers' concept of functionalism. The dairy wing, erected in the 1930's to house additional cattle, is now used as winter quarters for some of the village's farm animals. This dairy wing, with its twin wooden Unadilla Silos and Louden barn fittings, is an indication that farming was of primary importance to the Hancock Shakers.

(right) Interior framing of Round Stone Barn showing the central ventilating shaft
(below) Round Stone Barn exterior

(above) 1885 view of Hancock brethren and dairy herd.
(right) Views of the Round Stone Barn before and during its 1968 restoration.

9

Tan House 1835

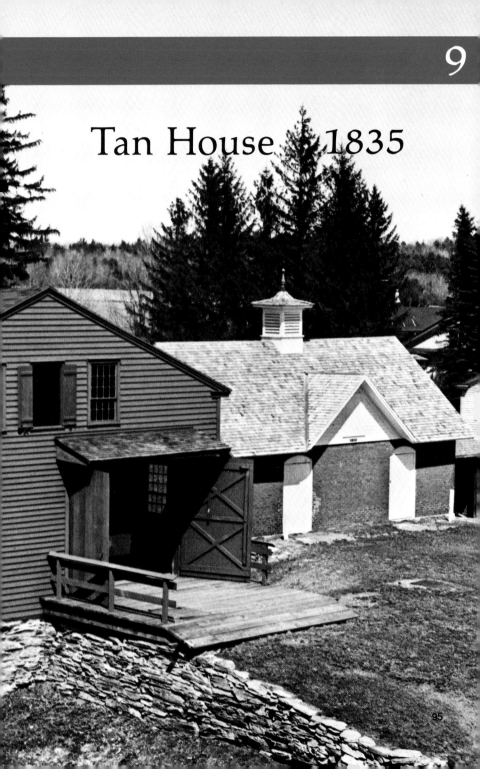

Erected in 1835 on the site of a former cider house, the Tannery, the second one erected by the Church Family, housed their flourishing leather industry which supplied the leather for the Shaker shoemakers, harnessmakers and hatters. A visitor in 1846 remarked: "... we look into various places the most important of which was the Tannery which is the best establishment of the kind I have ever seen."

The operation of the Tannery occupied the space of all three floors. Large cypress vats in the basement, fed by an adjacent cistern, held the hides while they were soaked, rinsed, and leached. In the room above, the pieces were scraped and later smoothed and softened with sticks, and in the attic hides were dried and stored. In 1860, the Tannery was listed as having capital invested of $2000 and an annual production of 600 sides of leather, 200 calfskins, 400 kips, and 510 sheep skins for a total value of $3128, a substantial sum for this one trade.

By 1875, the picture had changed considerably. The Tillotson Tannery Mill in nearby Pittsfield, which had been in operation for a number of years, had grown to the point where they could produce and handle leather more efficiently and cheaply than the Shakers.

The industry was therefore shortly abandoned and the building converted to other uses. The large vats from the tannery operation are still buried in the basement floor.

Among the new uses for the building were a smith shop which was moved in sometime after 1874, and a cider room to press the apples from the Shaker orchards. Baldwins, Wrights and Northern Spies were among the varieties grown by the Hancock Shakers. Cider was one of the primary beverages served at Shaker meals and was carried by the brethren into the fields to relieve their thirst. In a 1973 museum restoration of the building, an 1880's Dunning Boushort cider press was installed to replace a similar one which had been scrapped during World War II.

The rooms above the cider and smith shops were devoted to woodworking, carpentry, and milling activities. Clifford Peck, a farm hand at the Church Family until 1952, remembers the large grinding wheel, powered by a water turbine, which was on this floor. He used it often to sharpen axes, shovel blades, hoes, and other farm tools. Mr. Peck assisted in the restoration of this building in 1973, and his knowledge of mechanical skills helped to make the water turbine and line shafts once again operable.

The Shakers often used principles of physics to assist them in their work; two of these principles are utilized in this building. First, a windlass located in the attic was used to raise heavy loads with minimal effort. Secondly, they designed the underground cistern with sides that slope upward, smaller at the bottom than at the top, to allow for freezing ice to move upward rather than bursting the stone walls.

(preceding page) Southwest view 1835 Tan House
(top) Attic area of Tan House showing windlass or hoisting device.
(bottom) Line drawing of late 19th century water turbine.

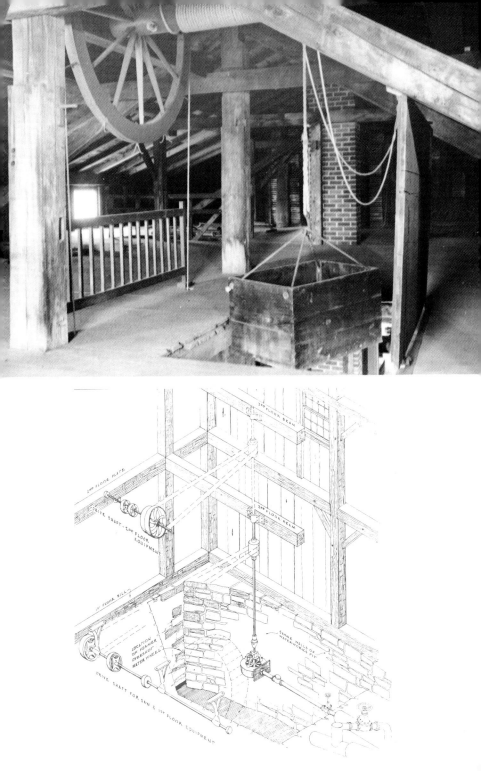

Ice House

The Shaker community, like its worldly neighbors, had a definite need for refrigeration to preserve its meats, vegetables, and dairy products. As early as 1844 the Shakers at Hancock had an Ice House, and by 1894, the need for a new one of improved design was felt. The Hancock correspondent to the *Manifesto,* the Shaker monthly magazine, described the new ice house in December 1894:

> We have long anticipated the possession of a new ice house, with modern improvements. Within the last two months, it has been erected. The building is 22 x 34 ft. with brick walls 18 ft. high, laid in red-colored mortar. One half of the lower story is finished inside with southern pine, to be for cold storage. The ice hall and chamber will hold about two hundred tons of ice. The outside woodwork is painted a light-gray color, and presents quite a nice appearance. There are rooms for vegetables, fruits, meats and many things that we may care to keep for a long or short time.

By 1927, the ice box had been replaced by the electric refrigerator and the need for an Ice House ceased. Never wasting space, the Shakers soon converted it into a milk house and so it went until the 1940's when its last days of family use saw it housing poultry.

(upper left) Southeast view of Ice House showing utilization of hillside for insulation
(left) Ice was harvested from the Shaker reservoir and stored in the chambers over and left of the cold storage rooms.

11

Brick Garage

In the opinion of the Shakers, the advent of the automobile was one of the great forward steps of modern technology. The first car purchased by the Church Family was a Cadillac. The garage, like the Brick Dwelling House, was built with future membership of the Society in mind, as indicated by the four bays of the garage. One of the practical features of the structure is the wraparound system of steam pipes installed to keep the car engines from freezing up in the severe Berkshire winters. The steam was supplied by insulated pipes carried overhead from the Hired Men's Shop next door. A 1919 newspaper account of a Shaker funeral notes:

> Among the finest cars seen at the Shaker funeral were those owned by the Shakers themselves. All the communities have them now. They go on the theory that the best is invariably the cheapest in the long run.

The Hancock Shakers were among the first in the Berkshires
to recognize the distinct advantages of the automobile.
The garage was built c. 1915.

Hired Men's Shop and Printing Office

I n 1905, a fire destroyed the Deacons' Shop located on this site, and Elder Ira Lawson ordered that an unused seed shop be moved from the north side of Route 20 to replace the building. It was used as living quarters and shop area for some of the hired men needed to work the farm. The use of hired men had increased as membership in the Society waned; in 1905, there were thirty-nine members in the Church Family at Hancock and fifteen hired men.

Today the rooms on the second floor portray the living quarters of the hirelings; the first floor houses a printing shop. Before 1812, Shaker publications had been done by commercial printers, but in that year Josiah Tallcott Jr., a member of the Second Family at Hancock, produced the first Shaker printed work. In 1813, he reissued this work, *Millennial Praises . . .,* as a complete book. Josiah Tallcott's second book, *Testimonies of the Life, Character, Revelations and Doctrines of Our Ever Blessed Mother Ann Lee, and the Elders with Her, . . .* (1816), is thought to have been printed in a small edition of only 20 copies making it one of the rarest of Shaker imprints.

By the twentieth century, hired men dominated the Shaker work force.

13

1880-1910-1939 Barn Complex

Hancock Shaker Village was primarily a farm community with many structures devoted to agricultural needs. This three-portion barn complex typifies the Shakers' acceptance of new ideas and equipment, especially those related to farming.

The first part of the complex is the long concrete and stucco horse, calf, and hay barn dated 1910. Originally built during the latter part of 1879 and finished in 1880, it was struck by lightning in 1910 and "burned down being full of hay and wagons at the time." This was the second time that a building on this site had burned; so when the Shakers began reconstruction in September 1910, they made several changes. The base stone foundation was repaired, and the first two stories were formed with plank and poured in concrete. The remaining two stories were framed and sheathed in wood, and the entire building was covered in stucco to give it a uniform appearance. As a last fire preventative, it was roofed with colored New Hampshire slate.

The ell of this complex was a dairy wing erected in 1939 to house an additional thirty head of Holsteins. This wing follows a building plan prescribed by the Louden Farm Machinery Company of Fairfield, Iowa. It was built by a Pittsfield contractor. The equipment shed extending from the north end was built in 1968 after the demolition of an earlier shed.

The first floor level of the concrete barn has a vaulted brick root cellar on the south end, buried beneath the wagon ramp to the upper hay loft. Potatoes, squash, turnips, and other root crops were kept through the winter here before the advent of refrigeration.

(top) Agricultural structures dominated the Shaker landscape
(bottom) Stereoptican view of the 1879 Shaker hay barn raising

(above) The Trustees Office
was the first stop
on a visit to Hancock

(left) Mrs. Edwards,
a Hancock visitor,
models a Shaker
bonnet and cloak.

14

Trustees' House
and Office

The order of office deacon or trustee was the second oldest established position in the hierarchy of the Shaker Society. In the year 1792, Daniel Goodrich Sr. and David Goodrich were appointed as the first trustees of the Church Family to regulate the trades and to care for all the lands, monies, and property of the family. These positions of trust, like the others in the Shaker Society, were soon to be shared equally between men and women. Among the responsibilities of the "office deacons" was the care of all persons who called or visited at the Church, Shaker and non-Shaker alike.

Hancock's first office, on the site of the present structure, was a small building erected shortly after the organization of the community. In about 1813 the present Trustees' House was built, though in a different form than it exists today.

In 1852, the decision was made to enlarge the office. At this time the roofline was changed and the building was extended about thirty-five feet to the south. In 1853, a Shaker sister recorded:

> The Ministry from Holy Mount New Lebanon came over for a visit we visited them at the office it being the first time they had ever been there since it was repaired. They took dinner in the new dining room; and they put their blessing upon every part of it.

A woodhouse was erected to the east of the building and a brick privy to the south, and an office barn to the rear of the new woodhouse was doubled in size.

The location of the house at the east end of the village proved ideal since most visitors came from the Shaker railway depot or the town of Pittsfield five miles to the east. One problem with the location was that the basement area where the kitchen was located was five feet below grade, and on several occasions the kitchen was completely flooded. In 1876, this problem was solved when the office and woodhouse were joined with a connecting wing of two stories and the first floor became the new kitchen.

Until 1895 the Office remained an example of classic Shaker architecture — completely symmetrical with matched double doorways and green blinds (or shutters) against white clapboard sides. An 1885 visitor described a visit to the house:

TRUSTEES OFFICE AND SALES ROOMS,

SHAKER VILLAGE, WEST PITTSFIELD.

All visitors to Pittsfield and Berkshire towns are invited to visit Shaker Village and examine our large and novel selection of FANCY GOODS, Ladies' and Children's Articles and an elegant line of Unique and Novel Goods, only to be found at the Shaker Village, Shaker Butter-nuts, Walnuts and Flag Root.

MARTHA JOHNSON & M. FRANCES HALL,
Salesladies and Managers.

Don't miss visiting and seeing the Shakers and their wares.

The Shakers, like their contemporaries, advertised their wares in local business directories as in this 1904 example.

(right) Back porch of the Trustees Office in the 1880's.

A small room contains the wares the Shakers here offer for sale, wax acorns, pin-cushions, yarn winders, books, photographs, dish mops, sugared nuts, and other simple things . . . all finding a ready sale, since the honesty of the Shakers is proverbial, and everything they make is sure to be as represented.

By the end of the nineteenth century with the population of the entire community at a low of fewer than fifty members, the decision was made to remodel the Office. The end result, in 1895, was far more than just a larger building; it was a high Victorian structure with a tower, palladian and bay windows, bracketed porches, awnings, and interior features such as flowered wallpaper and match board floors. No explanation was ever recorded as to why they decided on such an ornate remodeling, but it is probable that it was an attempt to change their image. If they could show visitors and passersby that this was a modern, up-to-date community, no longer averse to change, perhaps more people would be encouraged to join.

However, the days of growth were over. Visitors still called until the closing of the community in 1960, no longer for the products of the store, but rather for the furniture and other antiques which are still widely sought.

The final act carried out in the Office, which was the last occupied building in the Village, was the negotiation for the sale of the community to Shaker Community, Inc. Thus to the end, the temporal and legal matters of the Society were carried out according to Gospel order.

Today, a portion of the interior is open to visitors where they may see the Victorian embellishments added at the turn of the century.

The brick privy has been restored and the interior remodeled to accommodate modern public restroom facilities.

IN LOVING MEMORY
OF MEMBERS OF THE
SHAKER CHURCH
WHO DEDICATED THEIR LIVES
TO GOD AND TO THE GOOD OF
HUMANITY
PASSED TO IMMORTALITY

ERECTED BY THE
WEST PITTSFIELD AND HANCOCK MASS. COMMUNITY
IN THE YEAR
1943

15

Shaker Cemetery

Prior to 1813, the Hancock community had a common burying ground near the West Family, which probably had originally been a family lot begun by the Tallcotts, early members of the community. In 1813, when a fever swept the area and many brethren and sisters died, a new burial ground was established in this location.

During the mid-nineteenth century there were several instances of the reinterment of the remains of important earlier leaders of the Society. A Hancock Elder noted in 1854:

> The bones of Mother Sarah Harrison and Father Calvin (Harlow) were removed from the old burying ground near the West Family to the burying ground north of the Chh (Church) office. They had lain in their earthly resting place between 58 and 60 years and the coffins were in a remarkable state of preservation.

The funeral and burial practices of the sect, while not unique, were somewhat different from those of their contemporaries. Since the Shaker Church considered the soul primary, the physical remains were given only minimal concern. The 1860 edition of the Millenial Laws states: "It is sufficient to dress a male corpse in a shirt or shroud, a handkerchief, and a muffler, if necessary, and for a female add thereto a cap and collar."

The burial arrangements were usually the duty of either a family deacon or deaconess. The room of the dead person was usually repainted soon after the death. An eldress in 1867 notes: "Elder Thomas stays with Elder Wm. last night. Elder Wm. dies at 8 in the morning. Elder Fidilio makes the coffin I . . . help line the coffin." Once the body was washed and dressed it was placed in the meeting room where the family would pay its respects. Following a short service, it was carried to the cemetery on a bier. The burial itself was short; a few songs were sung and then the family usually went to the Meeting House for a short joyful service to wish the soul welcome in the spiritual heaven.

An excellent description of the cemetery was in a Pittsfield newspaper in 1896:

The central cemetery monument, silhouetted against Mt. Sinai, the community's holy mountain.

There are probably 250 graves in this little yard, and they are all arranged in rows with the regularity of a chalk and plumb line, and at the head of each grave is a small plain marble slab, a little over two feet tall and a little more than a foot wide, and of those 250 slabs, less than a dozen are in any way ornamental, all of the others being practically identical as to size, shape and general appearance. On none of the marks of the graves of the Shakers is there anything concerning the life of the one whose resting place it marks, save the name, the date of death and the age...No fine gravel walks lead up to this 'city of the dead' and no winding paths pass in and out among the graves; yet all is neat, and its extreme simplicity renders it attractive. In one corner by themselves are a few graves with markers a little more pretentious than those of the great majority, and they are evidently those of persons who in life were not of the Shaker faith, but in death found a resting place among them.

(from left to right) Mother Sarah Harrison, first female leader of Hancock appointed in 1790; typical example of early stone showing only initials, age, and date of death; Joseph Wicker, chief spiritual medium during the period of Mother Ann's work; Louis Basting, last male minister and elder of the Hancock community.

In June 1943, the small tombstones were removed and a single monument raised in its place which stands today. This was done with the encouragement of the central ministry at Mount Lebanon to honor equally all the members interred there.

Looking beyond the cemetery one sees Shaker Mountain or Mt. Sinai, in the distance. Here during the period of Mother Ann's work, a time of intense spiritual revival among the Believers, a portion of the peak was cleared for a feastground and a fountain stone erected. On selected Sundays and other occasions specified by the elders, outdoor worship services were held during which the members communicated with God, Mother Ann, and other members of the spirit world. The restoration of Mt. Sinai is one of the long range projects of the museum.

16

Schoolhouse

Shortly after the gathering of the community in 1791, a school was established for the children in the Shaker families. On April 7, 1800, it was set off as a separate school district by the Town of Hancock and in 1817, became a public school available to local children as well as Believers. Soon a second school was established since part of the community lay within the bounds of West Pittsfield. The Shaker schools, with a brother or sister as teacher, were generally well regarded, although the subjects taught were limited to "reading, writing, a little arithmetic, a little grammar, and a little geography." An 1839 Pittsfield School Committee Report states:

> The school in the Shaker district has been taught with great fidelity and system and has been a pattern of regularity, quietness, and good behavior. The improvement in all the classes has been uniform and good, but not as great as in other schools. The probable reason for this circumstance is to be found in the fact that the scholars receive only about three months schooling a year. The boys are taught in the winter and the girls in the summer. With larger schools we might easily anticipate an amount of improvement here fully equal to any within the circle of our experience.

By 1896 the curriculum was more diversified. A newspaper account noted: "In addition to the routine work usually found in such schools, is taught free hand drawing and the children are given some practical instructions in botany, music, calisthenics, etc." The article also said that the pupils "are quite a little in advance of those in the city."

While the actual date of construction of the Schoolhouse is not known, an 1820 map of the Village shows it, but it was drawn in after the completion of the original map. Structural research, recently carried out, indicated through construction techniques, hardware, and clapboard size a probable 1820-1830 date of origin.

Sister Olive Hayden Austin, who entered the Society in 1903 at age seven, spent seven years in school in this building. She recounted:

(top) The Shaker school still housed a class of six students as late as 1925
(bottom) Children from surrounding communities often attended the highly respected Shaker school

. . . the school had twenty individual seats in four rows of five. The teacher's desk sat on a raised platform on the right with the superintendent's chair next to it and a melodian on the opposite side. A big pot-bellied stove in the front of the room had a pipe that ran all the way to the back of the room and into the chimney. There were two doors to enter the school, the one on the east side was for the teacher to enter her washroom and where the books were stored, ours was on the opposite side with a small hall lined with pegs to hang our coats on and a large woodbox we children had to keep filled. Boys and girls each had their own privy behind the school, the boys on the left and the girls on the right.

Sometime in the 1930's the Schoolhouse was closed, and the few remaining children moved into a room in the Brick Dwelling House. The last photograph of the building in place was taken in 1934; shortly thereafter it was sold, moved, and converted into a small house. In 1940 the closing of the Shaker school was mentioned in the Hancock town report: "This course was deemed advisable as the Shakers had decided not to care for any more children of school age. Also . . . there are no more children of school age in this part of the town."

In 1976, the Village built a reconstruction of the Shakers' Schoolhouse on its original site in order to interpret the important part that education played in the life of a Shaker community.

This 1870 clock face with movable
hands was used as a teaching aid.

Horse Barn

Another of the many buildings devoted to the care and housing of live-stock, this Horse Barn was raised by the brethren on June 5, 1850. In later years the barn was referred to as Elder Louie's barn; Elder Louis Basting who had moved to Hancock in 1887 used it for the horses and driving carriages of the ministry.

The Horse Barn was restored in 1974 and used for several years as an educational center for visiting school children. In 1984, the Village's expanding farm necessitated reclaiming the building for agricultural uses. Presently it provides housing for work horses, wagons, tools, and equipment used on the farm.

The Horse Barn housed the carriage horses for the Church Family Ministry.

Ministry Shop

The function of the ministry in relation to the families at Hancock was that of overall supervision of their spiritual and temporal well being. The ministry, as defined by the Shakers in their work *The Millennial Church,* are "As faithful ambassadors of Christ . . . invested with wisdom and authority, by the revelation of God, to guide, teach and direct his church on earth, in its spiritual travel, and to counsel and advise in other matters of importance, whether spiritual or temporal." They are given "the power to appoint ministers, elders and deacons, and to assign offices of care and trust to such brethren and sisters as they shall judge to be best qualified for the several offices to which they have been assigned."

The Hancock ministry had the further charge of the communities at Enfield, Connecticut, and Tyringham, Massachusetts, under what was termed a "bishopric." This added responsibility kept the ministry constantly on the move between their charges. Even with their extra duties, the laws of the sect required these leaders to perform some type of manual labor.

Because of their rank, special buildings were erected for their use. Lamson notes in 1847 that the upper story of the Meeting House served as the living quarters for the ministry and "at the East of this are two buildings, two stories high each. These are the ministry's work shops. One for the two brethren, and the other for the two sisters. If the elders have any business with the ministry, they may call at their shops."

By 1850 all references to the two ministry's shops end. After this date it appears that one structure, the elders' shop, was used by both sexes, and the eldresses' shop was converted to use as a garden seed house for this expanding industry. The shop was used until the spring of 1873, when a visiting elder from Canterbury reported:

> After breakfast we accompanied Elder Thomas to the Ministry's Shop, which was moved from its foundation & now rested on blocks. This old building they intend to sell and will immediately commence the building of a new shop on the spot where the former one stood.

This building was used by the Hancock ministry until its dissolution on June 18, 1893, and thereafter by the New Lebanon ministry of Daniel Offord, Levi Shaw, Harriet Bullard, and Augusta Stone.

Descriptions of the elders and eldresses at work are abundant. An example from 1869 states:

We found Elder Thomas Damon to be a universal genious and Mechanic his shop bore marks of this unmistakeable character throughout. He has built an ingenious turning lathe for turning Iron, which is a most complete specimen of workmanship, and has constructed machinery for cutting out and dressing up the various parts of the kind of swifts that are screwed to a table for use, which does the business most completely. He is the inventor of these swifts and manufactures them by the wholesale at 50 cts per pair, and was at this time filling an order for 20,000 pair at that rate. Several of the Sisters were aiding in this Job, at such parts as they could perform, which were not a few.

In its last year of use, the building served as the home of the Shakers' hired caretakers. It was restored in 1968 following a fire that destroyed the rear wing which had been used as a carpentry and cabinet shop.

The Ministry Shop was the work area for the spiritual leaders of the Hancock bishopric.

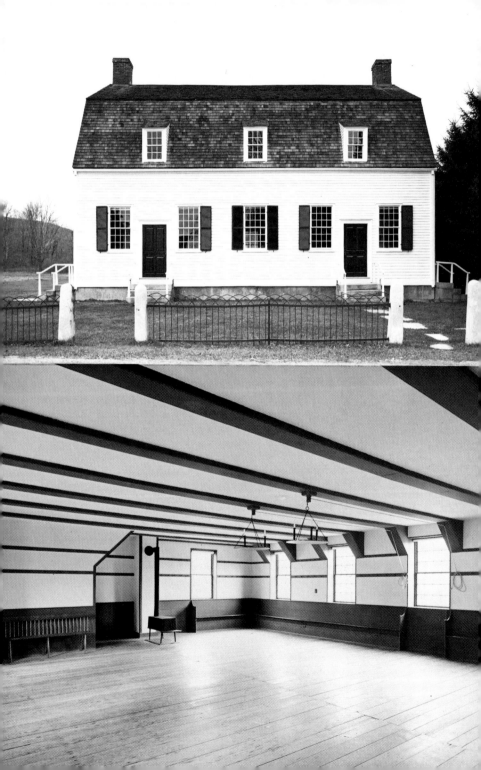

19

Meeting House

In every community the one building which stood in prominence above all others was the meeting house or church, from whence the Church Family derived its name. It served as the place of worship for all the families of the entire community on the Sabbath. The present building is the second building to occupy the site, and was originally located at the Shaker community at Shirley, Mass. It was moved to Hancock in 1962.

The original Meeting House with its gambrel roof was begun on August 30, 1786, five years before the Church Family was officially organized, indicating the strong sense of commitment by the people in this place to the new Society. One year after the Meeting House at New Lebanon was raised, Moses Johnson, a Believer from Enfield, New Hampshire, who "was an expert in hewing timber, and skilled in framing for building purposes" was assigned the task of framing the church at Hancock.

A traveler in 1817 recorded that the building was:

> . . . of beautiful workmanship, painted inside a glossy Prussian blue, the steps at the door are hewn out of a solid block of white marble, and from the neatness of everything one would suppose the whole house was washed between every meeting day . . . There are no fixed seats or pews in the meeting house, but only movable benches.

Elder Henry Blinn of Canterbury refers to the church at Hancock several times in his journals. In 1853, he states: "The Meeting House is the original one & would hardly be known from those in other societies, as they were all built of an exact size and one pattern." Later in the year on another visit he remarks:

> The meeting house . . . remains in its primitive form. It is the cause of reflection or it sometimes produces reflection, when we see such splendid & costly edifices reared in the different societies for our personal accommodation, while the house dedicated solely to God, is left & seemingly uncared for through all the changes that may occur . . . However, the worship of God is not wholly confined to one particular building, but the soul of the devout Believer is mindful of his duty at all times and in all places.

(top) The Meeting House, only used on Sundays, had separate doors for the brethren and sisters.
(bottom) The large open meeting room provided unobstructed space for the Shakers' dancing services
(overleaf) Four stages in the re-erection of the Shirley, Massachusetts Meeting House at Hancock in 1962

The first mention of the community's use of the Meeting House came in 1790. In 1817, a visitor discussed a service there:

The floor being quite clean, they all kneel to a silent prayer, on the right knee. Then they rise and form in regular columns, the men on one side, the women on the other. Several men and women then commence a tune, while every other person dances, keeping time admirably for at least half an hour. The men and women facing each other, advance and recede a few steps alternately, through the performance. When dancing is over, the seats are placed and an exhortation begins; — after sitting a short time, they rise and join in singing a hymn; then they take their seats and another exhortation follows, that generally concludes the meeting.

The maintenance and care of the Meeting House was handled by people from all the families. In 1850, Elder Thomas Damon of the Church Family noted:

. . . painted the meeting house and ministry shop twice the out stairs and fence by the road once. All performed by ourselves he and Elder Grove Wright without any foreign aid.

Cleaning of the Meeting House was a responsibility of the sisters of the various families, and changes and improvements were the responsibility of the families themselves. An example was in 1870 when the West Family turned over a piece of land to the Church Family, which was to be sold and the proceeds used for improvements to the structure. These were carried out and soon the old gambrel roof had been changed to a gable so that the building was a full two stories in height.

The change in appearance had little effect on Hancock's declining membership. In 1893, with the dissolution of the Hancock ministry, control over the Society was placed under the Mount Lebanon ministry, and the building fell into disuse. Finally, after forty-five years of abandonment, the structure was razed in 1938.

The Church at Hancock was to have, in another twenty-four years, a nearly identical Meeting House, framed by the same builder, Moses Johnson. The Shirley, Mass., meeting house, acquired from the State of Massachusetts for the price of one dollar, has a history nearly equal to that of Hancock, although it had been erected a few years later, in 1792-93. A 1795 account of it stated:

We first viewed the meeting house, which drew our attention, because beautifully painted white on the sides & even over the roof. The doors were green. Within, the wood work is painted of a deep blue, & the seats are of a chocolate color . . .''

His description is detailed, even to a description of the lighting devices, which were a flat plate on which candles could be set; the whole arrangement could be pulled up or down.

Today the Meeting House, with interpreters presenting daily programs of Shaker music, is one of the focal points of the Village. The apartments of the ministry on the second floor interpret the plain lifestyle of these leaders.

20

Garage

The small two-bay Garage was originally part of a wood house which served the three-story Sisters' Shop and store built in 1869 and taken down in 1958. This woodshed, built at the same time, was remodeled about 1910 to house the Shaker automobiles.

A group of Shaker children photographed near the Garage.

Laundry and Machine Shop

Duradecades of the Church Family's existence, funds for the erection of specialized buildings for separate activities and for each sex were not available. This building was divided in half and the brethren operated a heavy machine shop in the eastern end, while the sisters had their laundry and ironing rooms in the western section.

According to tradition, the earliest parts of the structure were built in 1790, with a series of additions put on over the next eighty years. The Machine Shop was located here because it was directly in line with the Shaker pond or reservoir, from which water was gravity fed through iron pipes to a large overshot wheel located in the basement. From this wheel the water was conveyed underground to the washing rooms and stables.

Most of the work carried on here would be classified as heavy mill work, such as the cutting and planing of lumber, the turning of large pieces of wood on lathes, and the machining of metal fittings and pieces for various purposes. Mechanics such as John Patten, Elder Thomas Damon, and Elder Ira Lawson spent large portions of their time busily at work in these shops.

As use of the building grew, and more machinery was added, the efficiency of the large water wheel declined. In December 1858, Thomas Damon noted that he had "sent to J.R. Clarke of Cohoes for plans and drawings of this improved turbine to take the place of the 20 foot overshot wheel at the Church Hancock agreeing to give him $15.00 for the same." During the next two years, the whole water power system was improved with the introduction of several varieties of water turbines, cast iron boiler flues used as water pipes, and a new type of line shaft and bearings.

In later years, use of the shop was generally limited to cutting cord wood for the many Shaker stoves, and after the death of Ira Lawson in 1905, it saw little or no use at all.

The wash house or Laundry cared for by the sisters was in operation shortly after 1800. As in most other areas of domestic practice, there were rules for washing and ironing. At Hancock in 1841, Eldress Cassandana Goodrich recorded a version of these. Rule one began:

(top) Water piped into this building provided both power and washwater for the family.
(bottom) Growing and processing medicinal herbs was one of the Shakers first and most profitable industries.

Sort your clothes and put every sort and kind together . . . And whether you wash with soda or without it, have your clothes washed clean, boiled and rinsed well. This with a little blueing will make them look very well . . . After the washing is finished, clean the tubs, pails and dippers . . . Don't forget to be prudent of soap.

While seemingly tedious in tone, the rules were meant as words of wisdom to aid in efficient operation and insure that work begun in the morning was completed by supper.

Sisters on laundry duty, like those in the kitchen, were rotated every few weeks to insure that each shared equally in the work.

Today the second floor of the Machine Shop serves as an exhibit area devoted to the herb and garden seed industry. Begun by the Church Family before 1800, the original Garden Seed House was erected to the west of this building, and used for the preparation, sorting, and packaging of seeds for sale to the world. Garden seeds from Hancock were among the best produced by Believers and were its most valuable industry. In 1839, a typical year, printed seed lists showed sixty-nine varieties of vegetable seeds. This was also the year of the great seed robbery which is a good example of the value of the industry. On Feb. 16, 1839, "the Garden Seed House was broken open by a band of robbers, and property taken to the amount of $3,325. This amount is estimated by recounting the seeds all papered & then deducting 25 per cent." At six cents a packet, this is an enormous sum. The value of this property, later recovered, led to the posting of a $400 reward notice and the eventful capture of one Lewis Wheeler on the 25th of June.

The garden seed industry was carried on at Hancock until sometime after 1885, when declining membership and business forced its discontinuance.

The last of the related industries is that of the preparation of dried green sweet corn. Hancock marketed this product through the East and Second Families as well as the Church until 1920. Put up in tin-lidded, bent wood containers it was a popular Pittsfield product sold chiefly through the Howard Seed Store on North Street.

$400 Reward.

The Seed Store of the subscribers

was broken open, at Hancock Shaker Village, on Saturday night, the 16th inst. and property to the amount of from One Thousand to Two Thousand Dollars stolen therefrom; consisting principally of Garden Seeds. Also 4 Baskets, 12 Meal Bags, and 1 pair Patent Double Beam Scales.

$200

Will be paid by the subscribers, upon the conviction of the Thief or Thieves in any Court of Justice, and

$200

Upon the recovery of the stolen property.

Joseph Patten, } *Trustees of*
Joseph Wicker, } *the*

Hancock, Feb. 18, 1839.   *United Society of Shakers.*

1839 Shaker reward poster for recovery of Hancock seed store property.

NOTICE.

IN consequence of the increasing amount of company to which we are at all times subject, it becomes necessary to adopt the following

RULES FOR VISITORS.

FIRST. We wish it to be understood that we do not keep a Public House, and wish to have our Rules attended to as much as any one would the rules of their own private dwelling.

SECOND. Those who call to see their Friends or Relatives, are to visit them at the Office, and not to go elsewhere, except by permission of those in care at the office.

THIRD. Those who live near and can call at their own convenience are not expected to stay more than a few hours ; but such as live at a great distance, or cannot come often, and have near relatives here, can stay from one to four days, according to circumstances. This we consider sufficient time, as a general rule.

FOURTH. All Visitors are requested to rise to take Breakfast at half past Six in the Summer, and half past Seven in the Winter.

FIFTH. At the Table we wish all to be as free as at home, but we dislike the wasteful habit of leaving food on the plate. No vice is with us the less ridiculous for being in fashion.

SIXTH. Married Persons tarrying with us over night, are respectfully notified that each sex occupy separate sleeping apartments while they remain. This rule will not be departed from under any circumstances.

SEVENTH. Strangers calling for meals or lodging are expected to pay if accommodated.

UNITED SOCIETY,

Picture Credits

Shaker Village, Inc.; **102** (top) Paul Rocheleau, (bottom) Williams College Library; **104** (top) Emma King Library, (bottom) Library, Hancock Shaker Village, Inc.; **106-107,** Library, Hancock Shaker Village, Inc.; **108,** Paul Rocheleau; **110-111,** Philip Lief; **112** (top) Photographer unknown, Elsie M. Christensen, owner; (bottom) Emma King Library; **114,** Philip Lief; **115-118** Paul Rocheleau; **120** (both) Joel Librizzi, *Berkshire Eagle,* Pittsfield, Mass.; **121** (top) Joel Librizzi, (bottom) Jack E. Boucher, Historic American Buildings Survey, Washington, D.C.; **123** (both) Library, Hancock Shaker Village, Inc.; **124** (both) Paul Rocheleau; **127,** Paul Rocheleau; **128,** Library, Hancock Shaker Village, Inc.; Guide Map, Terry F. Hallock.

Acknowledgements

Many people have helped in the preparation of this study. I wish to thank especially Mary L. Richmond for her generous help with source material, editing, and encouragement; Philip Lief for his design expertise; Paul Rocheleau for his excellent photographs; and two former Hancock sisters, Olive Hayden Austin and Evelyn Griffin Derby for their invaluable information about life at Hancock during their years in community. The staffs of the libraries which I visited for this study were most helpful, especially those at Western Reserve Historical Society, the Henry Francis du Pont Winterthur Museum, and the Shaker Museum at Old Chatham. I deeply appreciate the help of the following people: E. Ray Pearson, Charles E. Thompson, Eldress Gertrude Soule, Eldress Bertha Lindsay, Sister Miriam Wall, Robert F.W. Meader, William L. Lassiter, the staff of the Cooperstown Graduate Programs, Donald E. Richmond, James Daly Tobin, Amy Bess Miller, Sandra Scace, Martha Dahlen, Caren Hoffman. Special thanks are also due to Edward Deming Andrews, Faith Andrews, and Eugene Merrick Dodd for their valuable research into the Hancock Shakers. Above all, I wish to thank my wife, Lili Reineck Ott, for her untold patience, time and assistance in producing this work.

Bibliography

Books

Adams, Hannah. *A View of Religions.* 3rd. ed. Boston: Manning and Loring, 1801.

Andrews, Edward Deming. *The Community Industries of the Shakers.* Albany: The University of the State of New York, 1932.

_____. *The Gift to be Simple: Songs Dances and Rituals of the American Shakers.* New York: Dover Publications, Inc., 1962.

_____. *The Hancock Shakers.* Hancock: Shaker Community, Inc., 1961.

_____. *The People Called Shakers.* New York: Dover Publications, Inc., 1963.

Authorized Rules of The Shaker Community. Shaker Village, New Hampshire: Mount Lebanon Shakers, 1894.

Bentley, William. *The Diary of William Bentley.* Glouster, Mass.: Peter Smith, 1962.

(Bishop, Rufus, and Wells, Seth Y.). *Testimonies of the Life Character, Revelations and Doctrines of Our Blessed Mother Ann Lee, and The Elders with her; Through Whom the Word of Eternal Life Was Opened in this Day of Christ's Second Appearing.* Hancock: By Order of The Ministry, 1816.

_____. *Testimonies of the Life...*2nd ed. Albany: Weed, Parsons & Co., 1888.

Brown, Thomas. *An Account of the People Called Shakers: Their Faith, Doctrines, and Practice, Exemplified in the Life Conversations, and Experience of the Author During the Time He Belonged to the Society...*Troy, N.Y.: Parker and Bliss, 1812.

Business Directory of Berkshire County, Massachusetts, 1884-85. Syracuse: Hamilton Child, 1885.

Commonwealth of Massachusetts. *Acts and Resolves of the Legislature of Massachusetts in the Years 1839, 1840, 1841, 1842.* Boston: Dutton and Wentworth, 1842.

County of Berkshire. *Berkshire County Census During the Year Ending June 1, 1860.* Pittsfield: Brown and Cott, 1860.

Crosman, Charles F. *The Gardener's Manual...in the United Society at New Lebanon, Pittsfield, and Watervliet.* New Lebanon: by the Shakers, 1835.

A Declaration of the Society of People Commonly called Shakers. Albany: E. & E. Hosford, 1815.

Desroche, Henri. *The American Shakers From Neo-Christianity to Presocialism.* Amherst; The University of Massachusetts Press, 1971.

Dixon, William Hepworth. *New America.* 3rd ed. Philadelphia: J.B. Lippincott and Co., 1867.

Field, David Dudley. *A History of the Town of Pittsfield, in Berkshire County, Massachusetts.* Hartford: Case, Tiffany and Burnham, 1844.

Gates, Paul W. *The Farmer's Age: Agriculture 1815-1860*. New York: Harper and Row, 1968.

(Green, Calvin and Wells, Seth Y.). *A Brief Exposition of the Established Principles of the United Society of Believers, Called Shakers*. 8th ed. New York: E.S. Dodge, 1879.

_____. *A Summary View of the Millenial Church, or United Society of Believers (Commonly Called Shakers) Comprising the Rise, Progress and Practical Order of the Society...*Albany: by Order of the Ministry, 1823.

Guild, William. *A Chart and Description of the Boston and Worcester and Western Railroads*. Boston: Bradbury & Guild, 1847.

Hazard, Rodman. "A History of the Town of Hancock" in *A History of the County of Berkshire, Massachusetts by Gentlemen in the County, Clergymen and Laymen*. Pittsfield: Samuel W. Bush, 1829.

Hedrick, Ulysses Prentiss. *A History of Agriculture in the State of New York*. New York: Hill and Wang, 1966.

Hinds, William Alfred. *American Communities...*Oneida, New York: Office of the American Socialist, 1878.

Holland, Josiah Gilbert. *History of Western Massachusetts the Counties of Hampden, Hampshire, Franklin, and Berkshire*. Springfield: Samuel Bowles & Co., 1855.

Lamson, David R. *Two Years' Experience Among the Shakers: Being a Description of the Manners and Customs of That People...*West Boylston, Massachusetts: by the author, 1848.

Lassiter, William L. *Shaker Architecture*. New York: Bonanza Books, 1964.

MacLean, J.P. *A Bibliography of Shaker Literature with an Introductory Study of the Writings and Publications Pertaining to Ohio Believers*. Columbus: for the author by Fred J. Heer, 1905.

Macrae, David. *The Americans at Home*. New York: Dutton, 1952. (first published Edinburgh, 1870).

Melcher, Marguerite Fellows. *The Shaker Adventure*. Cleveland, Ohio: Western Reserve Historical Society, 1960.

*Millenial Praises Containing a Collection of Gospel Hymns...*Hancock: J. Talcott, 1812.

Nordhoff, Charles. *The Communistic Societies of the United States; From Personal Visit and Observation*. New York: Harper and Brothers, 1875. (reprinted Hilary House Publishers, Ltd., 1960).

Noyes, John Humphrey. *History of American Socialisms*. New York: Hillary House Publishers, Ltd., 1961.

One Hundredth Anniversary of the Organization of the Shaker Church Enfield, New Hampshire October 18, 1893. Enfield: Abbott's Power Print, 1893.

Robinson, Charles Edson. *A Concise History of the United Society of Believers Called Shakers*. East Canterbury, New Hampshire: Shaker Village, 1893.

The Round Stone Barn A Short History. rev. ed. by John Ott. Hancock: Shaker Community, Inc., 1975.

Smith, J.E.A. *The History of Pittsfield, (Berkshire County) Massachusetts from the Year 1800 to the Year 1876*. Springfield: C.W. Bryan & Co., 1876.

Warder, W.S. *A Brief Sketch of the Religious Society of People Called Shakers.* London, 1818.

Wells, Seth Y. *Testimonies Concerning the Character and Ministry of Mother Ann Lee and the First Witnesses...*Albany: Packard and Van Benthuysen, 1827.

White, Anna, and Taylor, Leila S. *Shakerism Its Meaning and Message Embracing An Historical Account, State-ment of Belief and Spiritual Experience of the Church from Its Rise to the Present Day.* Columbus. Ohio: Fred J. Heer, 1905.

Manuscripts

Each manuscript entry is keyed to its location: WML for the Henry Francis duPont Winterthur Museum Library, Winterthur, Delaware: OC for Emma B. King Library, Shaker Museum, Old Chatham, New York; WRHS for Western Reserve Historical Society, Cleveland, Ohio; HSV for Hancock Shaker Village, Pittsfield, Massachusetts; BA for Berkshire Atheneum, Pittsfield, Mass.; NYSL for New York State Library, Albany.

Account Book or Minnuit Book No 7 Jehiel Markham, Hancock, Mass. 1786-1788. WML 887.

An Account of the Building of the Brick Shop 1829 Mt. Lebanon. WRHS II, 36.

Agreement between David Terry and John Low regarding the rights to dig for mines and minerals, May 18, 1857, OC 9624.

Apprenticeship Agreement Between Ann Swift of Hancock, Mass. and David Terry Elder of the West Family Hancock, June 5, 1861. WML 876.

Basting, Louis. A. Sketch of the Early History of Pittsfield. April 1888. WML 808.

A Bill of Articles given to James Farnams family, at the time the House burnt in the fall of 1830. WML 938.

Bonet Expense Sheet 1854. WML 933.2

Book of the Busy Hours Commenced March 1 and June 23 1877. HSV.

A Book of Records Kept by Daniel Goodrich. 1794-1824. HSV.

A Christian Community by Henry Blinn of the Canterbury Shakers. HSV.

Circular Concerning the Dress of Believers from the Ministry Mt. Lebanon, New York. 1866. BA.

Collection of Hancock Seed Lists. Harvard School of Business Administration, Cambridge, Mass.

A Concise Statement of the Principles of the Only True Church According to the Gospel of the Present Appearance of Christ...1790. HSV.

Concise Statements Concerning the Life and Religious Views of the Shakers (1897). HSV.

Copies of Letters from various societies 1807-1864 sent to South Union, Kentucky for the Ministry, recopied in the book by Nancy E. Moore. WRHS.

The Covenant or Constitution of the Church at Hancock. 1830. OC 13602.

The Covenant or Constitution of the Second Family in the Hancock United Society residing in Pittsfield. April 5, 1832. OC 13601.

The Covenant or Constitution of the West Family in the Hancock United Society. Jan. 1, 1851. OC 13603.

Declaration of the Instruments in the Church Hancock. BA.

Deed for three parcels of property belonging to Jacob Adams and being sold to the Hancock Shakers July 2, 1829. WML 850. 1-2.

Dairy of a Journey from Canterbury, N.H. to Enfield and on to Lebanon, N.Y. and to Hancock, Mass. in a Carriage. June 14, 1853 begun. OC 12792.

Diary of the Ministry's Journey to New Lebanon and Groveland via Worcester, Pittsfield and Hancock . . . and Dairy of a Journey to New Lebanon in a Carriage, 1856. OC 12792.

Diary 1867 Eldresses in the Hancock Ministry. WML 797.

Early Book of Records of the Hancock Church Family 1789-1801. OC 10804.

Family Records — 2nd Family — Hancock. 1829-1877. WML 783.

Gardener's Journal. Sept. 1859-Nov. 1861. HSV.

Gardener's Journal of Various Things Commenced in AD 1842. 1842-1847. OC 10358.

Garden Seeds Raised at Hancock, Berkshire Co., Mass. and put up in Papers with the Retail Price Printed on them for Sale. 1821. HSV.

Goodrich, Cassandana. Mother's Pure Teaching — An Introduction to Good Rules. 1841-1845. WRHS 1b, 82.

Grove Wright's Book of Inspired Drawings 1841-1845. WML 1069.

Journal of an Anonymous Brother, Enfield, Conn. 1842-1846. WML 774.

Journal Containing Miscellaneous Dates Regarding the Construction of Buildings at New Lebanon, N.Y.; Hancock, Mass.; Enfield, Conn., and etc. 1822-1858. WML 841.

A Journal Continued to One Commenced Jan. 1st 1848 2nd Vol. July 21, 1850-Oct. 18, 1852. New Lebanon. OC 8831.

Journal of Domestic Events — Hancock. 1860-1863. WML 1053.

Journal: Elder William Williams Book — Hancock Feb. 8, 1840 WML 786.

Journal of Events. Hancock. 1818-1860. WML 782.

A Journal Kept by Grove Blanchard, Harvard, Mass. WRHS Vb, Vol. 48.

A Journal Kept by Lucy Hammond While on a Journey to New Lebanon, Hancock, Enfield in 1830. WRHS Vb, Vol. 39.

Journals of the Ministry of Harvard, Mass. Written in the Years 1844, 1845, and 1847. WRHS Vb, Vol. 51.

Journey of Philip Burlingame, Robert Aiker, Lucy Walton, Cassandana Benton, Margaret Hopkins, Aurelia Harriet Lyman to New Lebanon, Watervliet, Hancock, Tyringham from Enfield, Conn. 1856. WRHS Vb, Vol. 19.

Journal of Records Kept by Order of the Church. Vol. III. 1856-1871. OC 10342.

Journal of a Trip of the Harvard Ministry to New Lebanon, N.Y. and Hancock, Mass., Aug. 31-Sept. 16, 1840. Grove, Betty, Sally L. and John O. WRHS Vb, Vol. 49.

Journal of a Visit to Five Societies of Believers viz. Enfield, Conn., Tyringham and Hancock Mass. New Lebanon and Watervliet New York by a Company from Harvard in the Autumn of the Year 1846 . . . HSV.

Journal of Wealthy Storer, Tyringham and Hancock, Mass. 1846-1854. WML 789.

Leases for Rights to dig for iron ore on East Family Shaker Property. 1854 and 1867. WML 1552.1 and 1552.2.

Ledger — Seed Department. 1820-1836. Hancock, Massachusetts. OC 10446.

Letter from Sr. Alice M. Smith of Pittsfield, Mass. to Dr. Charles Adams of the New York State Museum. Office of State History, Rotterdam, New York.

Letter from the Ministry at Hancock, March 31, 1828. WML 1222.1.

Letter from the Ministry at Pleasant Garden (Shirley, Mass.) to Nathaniel Deming of the Ministry at the City of Peace. March 8, 1843. WML 1223.

Letters: Hancock Correspondence. WRHS IVa and b.

Letter from Pittsfield March 31, 1828 to Father Job. WML 1222.2.

Map: East Family West Pittsfield Shakers, A.W. Williams, Agent. Oct. 13, 1880. WML 1559.

Map: Hancock Church Family 1820 (Schematic). HSV.

Map of Property Belonging to the United Society Situated in Hancock, Pittsfield and Richmond. W.H. Barnes, Surveyor. Housatonic, Mass. Nov. 1887. HSV.

Memoranda, & etc. Mostly of Events and Things which have transpired since the first of Jan. 1846. Verifax copy, HSV.

Memorandum of Agreement Between Hancock and Pittsfield Shaker Communities and the Western Railroad Corporation. OC 9617.

Millenial Laws or Gospel Statutes and Ordinances adapted to the Days of Christ's Second Appearing . . . Recorded at New Lebanon, Aug. 7th, 1821. Revised and re-established by the Ministry and Elders, Oct. 1845. WRHS 1b, Vol. 17-18.

Mount Lebanon Church Family Journal. 1858-1867. HSV.

Mount Lebanon Church Family Journal. 1910-1924. OC 8851.

Names of the Brethren and Sisters when we moved into the Brick House. December 19, 1831. WML 1544. .

Notes on the way while on a Journey to the State of Kentucky in the year 1873. OC 12791.

Persons at Hancock between the ages of 18 and 45 liable under the Conscription Law of Enrollment. WML 1547.

Pittsfield Mass. Assessors Field Book Records. 1790-1900. City Hall, Pittsfield, Mass.

Pittsfield Town Reports. 1830-1900. BA.

Postal History Information — Berkshire County, Massachusetts. 1789-1890. Harlan T. Ballard Collection. Oct. 8, 1968. B.A.

A Record of Appointments and Changes in the Ministry at Hancock. WML 1545.

Record Book of Miscellaneous Events. 1833-1899. OC 10345.

Record of Deaths — Hancock; Church, 2nd, East and South Families to 1896. OC 12719.

A Record of Divinely Inspired Communications and Messages 1841-1843. WML 1068.

A Record of the Meetings Held on Mt. Sinai, Mt. Horeb, and the Mt. of Olives. 1844. NYSL.

A Record of Messages and Communications given by Devine Inspiration in the 2nd, West and East Families at Hancock and Pittsfield. WML 1082.

Receipt for Cloth sent to Hancock to be Fulled. WML 1003.1.

Richmond, Mary L. Shaker Literature: A Bibliography . . . with Annotations.

Rules and Orders for the Church of Christ's Second Appearing Established by the Ministry and Elders of the Church Revised and Reestablished by the Same New Lebanon, N.Y. May 1860. HSV.

Scrapbooks of Shaker Related Newspaper Clippings. HSV, BA.

Scrapbooks of Shaker Related Newspaper Clippings. WRHS XIII, Vols. 47, 48 and 49.

Selections from Various Lists of Names and Ages of Members, Elders, Trustees and Deacons in the Various Communities of the United Society with some Obituary Lists Compiled from Original Manuscripts by William H. Cathcart 1912. BA.

A Short Sketch of our Journey to the East . . . Hancock, 1850. WML 791.

Sister's Diary. Hancock, Mass. 1854. WML 792.

Sister's Diary. Hancock, Mass. 1865. WML 795.

Sister's Diary. Pittsfield, Mass. 1862. WML 794.

Smith, Alice Mae. History of Our Home — Hancock. Copied Nov. 17, 1907. OC 13377.

Sums of Money sent from Hancock 1805-1818. WRHS 11a, Folder 17.

Town Reports, Hancock, Massachusetts. 1780-1830. Records Room, Hancock Town Hall, Hancock, Massachusetts.

Trustees Account Book, 2nd Family, West Pittsfield Shakers. March 1847-January 1849. HSV.

Trustees Account Book, 2nd Family, West Pittsfield Shakers. 1831-1846. HSV.

Valentine Rathbun's Discharge to son Valentine. March 21, 1792. WML 871.

Wright, William B. Manuscript Notebook on the Shakers with sketch map of the various families of the Hancock Shaker community. 1904. Williams College Library, Williamstown, Massachusetts.

Shaker Journals

The Shaker, 1871-72; 1876-77.

Shaker and Shakeress, 1873-75.

The Shaker Manifesto, 1878-82.

The Manifesto, 1883-99.

The Shaker Quarterly, 1961-

Periodicals

Andrews, Edward Deming. "The Shakers in a New World," *Antiques,* LXXII, No. 4 (October, 1957), 340-343.

_____. "The Shaker Manner of Building," *Art in America,* XLVIII, No. 3 (July, 1960), 38-45.

Brainard, Jessie M. "The Enfield Shakers," *The Connecticut Quarterly,* III, No. 4 (Oct.-Dec., 1897), 461-474.

Dodd, Eugene Merrick. "Functionalism in Shaker Crafts," *Antiques,* XCVIII, No. 4 (October, 1970), 588-593.

Hopping, D.M.C. and Watland, Gerald R. "The Architecture of the Shakers," *Antiques,* LXXII, No. 4 (October, 1957), 335-339.

Johnson, Clifton. "The Passing of the Shakers," *Old Time New England,* XXV, Nos. 1 and 2 (July and October, 1934), 3-20 and 49-66.

Peladeau, Marius B. "The Shaker Meetinghouses of Moses Johnson," *Antiques,* XCVIII, No. 4 (October, 1970), 594-599.

"The Shakers," *Frank Leslie's Illustrated Newspaper,* XXXVII, Nos. 936 and 937 (September 6 and September 13, 1873), 416-418 and 12-14.

"The Shakers," *Harper's New Monthly Magazine,* XV, (June-November, 1857), 165-177.

Upton, Charles W. "The Shaker Utopia," *Antiques,* XCVIII, No. 4 (October, 1970), 582-587.

Articles

Bierstadt, O.A. "The Shakers," *The Day Star* (New York), April 9, 1885.

"Fire," *The Pittsfield Sun* (Pittsfield, Mass.), April 30, 1868.

"Ira R. Lawson—Dies at the Age of 71," *The Berkshire Evening Eagle* (Pittsfield, Mass.), April 5, 1905.

Richards, George E. "Hancock and Lebanon Shaker Colonies on Verge of Dissolution," News Clipping, Emma B. King Library, Shaker Museum, Old Chatham, New York, 14889, Aug. 1, 1919.

"Shaker Barn," *The New Hampshire Journal* (Concord, New Hampshire), June 11, 1827.

"The Shaker Fire," *The Berkshire County Eagle* (Pittsfield, Mass.), Dec. 8, 1864.

"Shaker Mill Destroyed," *Springfield Republican* (Springfield, Mass.), April 8, 1915.

"The Shaker Military Fines," *The Albany Gazette* (Albany, N.Y.), Jan. 20, 1832.

"The Shakers," *The New York American* (New York), Feb. 12, 1825.

"The Shakers," *The New York Weekly Tribune* (New York), April 17, 1852.

"Shakers at Pittsfield, Mass.," *The Pittsfield Sun* (Pittsfield, Mass.), Aug. 14, 1834.

"Shaker Wealth Only an Illusion," *The Boston Sunday Herald* (Boston), Jan. 28, 1905.

Shaker Related Newspaper Clippings filed at the Berkshire Athenaeum, the Berkshire Eagle Newspaper Office, Emma B. King Library (Old Chatham, N.Y.), Hancock Shaker Village, Western Reserve Historical Society Library and the Winterthur Museum Library.

"Shakerville Way," *The Sunday Morning Call* (Pittsfield, Mass.), May 17, 1896.

"A Trip Down a Shaker Mine," *Springfield Republican* (Springfield, Mass.), Jan. 18, 1896.

"2,500 Acres for Sale in West Pittsfield," *The Sunday Morning Call* (Pittsfield, Mass.), Dec. 29, 1901.

Catalogues

Anthony's Standard Business Directory, 1903-1904 Representing the Progressive Up-to-Date Business Firms of Pittsfield and Selected Towns in Berkshire County Who Want Your Trade. Northampton, Mass.: Anthony Publishing Company, 1903.

The Louden Machinery Company General Catalogue No. 50, Issued April 1920. Fairfield, Iowa: The Louden Machinery Co., 1920.

Shaker: Furniture and Objects from the Faith and Edward Deming Andrews Collections Commemorating the Bicentenary of the American Shakers. Washington, D.C.: Published for the Renwick Gallery of the National Collection of Fine Arts by the Smithsonian Press, 1973.

The Shakers; Life and production of a community in the pioneering days of American. An exhibition by the "Neue Sammlung." Munich, Germany: Printed by Hans Holzinger, 1974.

Interviews

Clinton, Connecticut. Personal interviews with former Hancock sister Olive Hayden-Austin. February, 1975.

Pittsfield, Massachusetts. Personal Interview with former Watervliet, N.Y., sister Mrs. John H. Fairs. December 3, 1974.

Hancock and Pittsfield, Massachusetts. Personal interviews with Persis Wellington Fuller long time friend of the Hancock and Lebanon Shakers. 1970-1975.

Pittsfield, Massachusetts. Personal interviews with architect Terry Hallock, museum consultant and specialist in Shaker architecture.

Canterbury, New Hampshire. Personal interview with Eldress Bertha Lindsay of the Central Ministry on August 6, 1974.

Pittsfield, Massachusetts and Hancock Shaker Village, Hancock, Massachusetts. Personal interviews on numerous occasions with Amy Bess Miller, long time friend of the Shakers and President of Hancock Shaker Village, Inc. 1970-1975.

Pittsfield, Massachusetts. Clifford Peck was interviewed while working on the restoration of our Tan House. Mr. Peck had been a former Shaker farm hand at the Church Family from 1936 until 1941. April-June, 1973.

Pittsfield, Massachusetts. Personal interview with Ralph Scace a former hired man on the Hancock Shaker farm and one of the chief persons involved in stripping the buildings before the sale to Shaker Community, Inc., in 1960.

Pittsfield, Massachusetts and Canterbury, New Hampshire. Personal interviews with Eldress Gertrude Soule of the Central Ministry and a former Eldress at the Shaker Communities at Alfred and Sabbathday Lake, Maine. June 10, 1973, June 15, 1974 and August 6, 1974.

Pittsfield, Massachusetts. Personal interview with Roger Wellington, last undertaker for the Shaker families at New Lebanon, New York, and Hancock, Massachusetts. May, 1974.

Other Sources

Mansfield, Luther Stearns. (Reprint) "Glimpses of Herman Melville's Life in Pittsfield, 1850-1851: Some Unpublished Letters of Evert A. Duyckinck," *American Literature*, IX, No. 1 (March, 1937), 26-48.

Sommer, Margaret Van Alen Frisbee. (Thesis) *The Shaker Garden Seed Industry*. Orono: University of Maine, 1966.

Location of Shaker Communities

LEGEND

1. Watervliet, N.Y. 1787-1938
2. Mount Lebanon, N.Y. 1787-1947
3. Hancock, Mass. 1790-1960
4. Harvard, Mass. 1791-1919
5. Enfield, Conn. 1792-1917
6. Tyringham, Mass. 1792-1875
7. Canterbury, N.H. 1792-(active)
8. Shirley, Mass. 1793-1909
9. Enfield, N.H. 1793-1918
10. Alfred, Me. 1793-1931
11. Sabbathday Lake, Me. 1793-(active)
12. West Union (Busro) Ind. 1810-1827
13. South Union, Ky. 1811-1922
14. Watervliet, O. 1813-1900
15. Union Village, O. 1812-1910
16. Pleasant Hill, Ky. 1814-1910
17. Whitewater, O. 1824-1907
18. North Union, O. 1826-1889
19. Groveland, N.Y. 1836-1892
   (formerly Sodus Bay, N.Y. 1826-36)

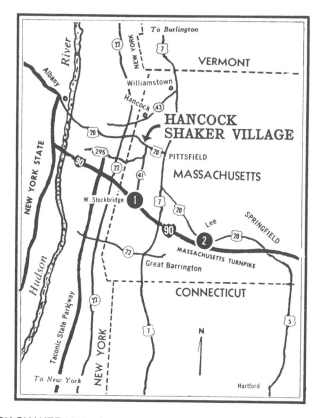

HANCOCK SHAKER VILLAGE is at the junction of Routes 20 and 41, five miles west of downtown Pittsfield in the Berkshire Hills of western Massachusetts. By automobile, the following are the best routes:

From New York and Albany: New York Thruway (Berkshire Spur) to Route 22; north on Route 22 to Route 295; east on Route 295 to Route 41; north on Route 41.

From Boston: Massachusetts Turnpike to Exit 1; north on Route 41.

From Taconic Parkway: East on Route 295 to Route 41; north on Route 41.

An alternate exit on the Massachusetts Turnpike is Exit 2 through Lee; north on Route 20 to Pittsfield; west on Route 20.

Important: Visitors approaching Hancock Shaker Village from the north via Routes 7 or 22 should note that it *cannot* be reached via Route 43 (to the Town of Hancock, from which the Village is separated by a mountain barrier) but should proceed to Route 20.

Friends of
Hancock Shaker Village

Membership Information

Hancock Shaker Village, Inc., is a non-profit educational organization. As such, the Village depends heavily on federal, state and local funds, as well as admission fees, the sale of publications and other items.

The Friends of Hancock Shaker Village have been an enduring source of financial support and volunteer effort. We invite you to join us.

Friends enjoy the following privileges:
- pride of being caretakers of the Shaker past as represented by the Village, its collections and diversified programs.
- free & unlimited admissions to the Village during the season.
- ten percent discount on items in the museum shop.
- advance notice of all special events, schedule of yearly workshops.
- Friends' Newsletter, mailed four times a year to keep you abreast of what's happening at the Village.
- opportunities, if you wish, to volunteer your time to assist in carrying out various Village programs.

For membership information, please contact:
Hancock Shaker Village, Inc.
P.O. Box 898
Pittsfield, MA 01202
(413) 443-0188

Programs at Hancock Shaker Village are funded in part by the Massachusetts Cultural Council, a state agency and the Institute of Museum Services, a federal agency.

Guide

Map Guide

1. Visitors' Center
2. Garden Tool Shed
3. Poultry House
4. Brick Dwelling House
5. Brethren's Shop
6. Sisters' Dairy and Weave Shop
7. Ministry Wash House
8. Round Stone Barn
9. Tan House
10. Ice House
11. Brick Garage
12. Hired Men's Shop and Printing Office
13. 1880-1910-1939 Barn Complex
14. Trustees' House and Office
15. Cemetery
16. Schoolhouse
17. Horse Barn
18. Ministry Shop
19. Meeting House
20. Garage
21. Laundry and Machine Shop